SECOND EDITION

Differentiated Assessment Strategies

*This book is dedicated to Marti Richardson, our colleague and friend.
Marti continues to inspire all educators to move toward their learning and leadership
potential through her enthusiasm and professional endeavors.*

SECOND EDITION

Differentiated Assessment Strategies

One Tool Doesn't Fit All

Carolyn Chapman · Rita King

CORWIN
A SAGE Company

FOR INFORMATION:

Corwin

A SAGE Company

2455 Teller Road

Thousand Oaks, California 91320

(800) 233-9936

Fax: (800) 417-2466

www.corwin.com

SAGE Ltd.

1 Oliver's Yard

55 City Road

London EC1Y 1SP

United Kingdom

SAGE India Pvt. Ltd.

B 1/I 1 Mohan Cooperative Industrial Area

Mathura Road, New Delhi 110 044

India

SAGE Asia-Pacific Pte. Ltd.

33 Pekin Street #02-01

Far East Square

Singapore 048763

Managing Editor: Cathy Hernandez

Associate Editor: Desiree Bartlett

Editorial Assistant: Kimberly Greenberg

Production Editor: Libby Larson

Copy Editor: Megan Markanich

Typesetter: C&M Digitals (P) Ltd.

Proofreader: Theresa Kay

Indexer: Terri Corry

Cover Designer: Rose Storey

Copyright © 2012 by Corwin

Printed in the United States of America.

Library of Congress Cataloging-in-Publication Data

Chapman, Carolyn, 1945-
Differentiated assessment strategies : one tool doesn't fit all / Carolyn

Chapman, Rita King.—2nd ed.

p. cm.

Includes bibliographical references and index.

ISBN 978-1-4129-9664-8 (pbk.)

1. Educational tests and measurements. 2. Individualized instruction. 3. Mixed ability grouping in education. I. King, Rita. II. Title.

LB3051.C4483 2012

371.26—dc23

This book is printed on acid-free paper.

11 12 13 14 15 10 9 8 7 6 5 4 3 2 1

Contents

PREFACE

FORMATIVE ASSESSMENT DATA ARE THE VITAL key to planning differentiated instruction. With this in mind, we designed this resource to assist teachers and administrators with the challenging, complex task of meeting learners' diverse needs. This guide to formative assessment can be used as a handbook by individual teachers or as a book study with a group of educators.

We strategically designed each strategy, template, checklist, and suggested guide for differentiated assessment. The activities can be created with materials found in classrooms. No extra resources or materials have to be purchased. Each formative assessment tool (1) is easily customized for the unique needs of individual learners, (2) provides immediate feedback for the teacher and learner, (3) produces data that do not require formal analysis, (4) can be used in all grade levels and subjects, and (5) is student and teacher friendly.

A seamless flow of assessment with data interpretation keeps the learner's identified needs in focus for the next steps in daily teaching. This saves time because specific needs are easily targeted and addressed. The strategies provide uncomplicated ways to continuously gather, monitor, record, and understand each learner's strengths and weaknesses. Using the informative tools, you can adjust daily plans and design interventions and enrichment to be sure each student is challenged with appropriate instruction.

Taking the advice of teachers and administrators in our training sessions, our colleagues and readers, we made many additions and improvements in this new edition. A new chapter addresses self-assessment. The approaches presented lead students to take ownership of the results and become responsible for their own learning. The assessment strategies to use before, during, and after learning are in three separate chapters to provide a treasure trove of ideas and techniques for your assessment toolbox. The strategies and tips are introduced and explained to create practical, intriguing assessment experiences.

THE GOALS OF THIS BOOK

Our goals in writing this teacher resource include the following:

- To provide a variety of differentiated formative assessment tools, strategies, and activities to identify a student's strengths and needs

- To emphasize the use of individual assessment data to guide each learner to mastery of identified standards

- To explore assessment strategies to use before, during, and after learning

- To apply differentiated planning models based on effective assessment

- To show how to interpret ongoing assessment data and use the results to design daily plans and personalize interventions

- To present novel, formative assessment tools that provide immediate feedback for teachers and learners

- To emphasize the value of creating a positive learning culture for assessment experiences

HOW THIS BOOK IS ORGANIZED

Chapter 1, One Tool Doesn't Fit All: Introduction, explores the key benefits of differentiated assessment. It emphasizes the importance of selecting the appropriate tool to use productively. Assessment terms are defined to provide a common language for readers.

Chapter 2, Bringing Research and Best Practices to Differentiated Formative Assessment, explores what the experts say about retaining information for long-term memory and for transfer. Approaches are explored to customize assessment experiences to make them personally meaningful for diverse learners.

Chapter 3, Creating a Climate for Formative Assessment, provides strategies, tips, and suggestions to establish a positive environment for assessment. The strategies are designed to instill individual self-efficacy in the affective domain of learning. The motivational benefits of using automaticity, "withitness," and risk-taking opportunities are emphasized.

Chapter 4, Knowing the Learner, examines the individual through different lenses or the many ways the student learns. Strategies are presented for educators to understand themselves, as well as the learner. These insights make it easier to select and plan differentiated assessments.

Chapter 5, Exploring Self-Assessment, provides exciting ways to engage learners in self-assessment. This chapter, new to this edition, explores ways for learners to become more responsible for their own learning. The strategies guide students to assess their learning experiences, analyze their personal needs, and identify their accomplishments.

Chapter 6, Formative Assessment Before the Learning, contains assessment tools to identify the student's background and knowledge related to a topic, concept, or skill. The learner's prior experience with a standard or skill is a prerequisite for planning differentiated instruction.

Chapter 7, Formative Assessment During the Learning, has a myriad of assessment tools to monitor student progress. This constant flow of information keeps the student on track. The strategies are designed for use by the teacher, individual students, partners, and small groups.

Chapter 8, Formative Assessment After the Learning, describes formative assessment tools for analyzing skills and the amount of information learned. The data provide a baseline for the next steps in daily planning or a valuable addition to the summative data.

Chapter 9, Differentiating Summative Assessments, examines strategies and techniques to accommodate the learner's needs during standardized tests. The chapter presents ways to use the test data to reach individual student's needs.

Chapter 10, Assessment for Differentiated Instruction and Flexible Grouping, explores differentiated instructional strategies as assessment tools. Some identified areas are technology, choice boards, cubes, and learning stations. Four basic ways to design assessment groups are presented with suggestions to create various grouping scenarios.

Chapter 11, Differentiated Instructional Planning Models, explores ways to use assessment data with five differentiated planning models to accommodate the learner. The models presented are Adjustable Assignment, Curriculum Compacting, Academic Contract, Project-Based, and Problem-Based.

Chapter 12, Planning for Differentiated Assessment, provides ideas to use in step-by-step planning. It includes a comprehensive checklist of all assessment tools presented in this resource. This handy guide can be used to select the most effective assessment strategies and to assess your implementation of and progress with formative assessment.

ACKNOWLEDGMENTS

WE DEEPLY APPRECIATE THE WORK OF EVERYONE ON THE staff at Corwin who contributed to the success of this resource. Cathy Hernandez, the managing editor, encouraged and supported us through each phase of the project. Megan Markanich, the copyeditor, enhanced our book with her work on our details and ideas. A special thank you to Libby Larson, the production editor, for her patience, expertise, advice, and gentle nudges during the final production stages.

Jim Chapman, Carolyn's husband, exhibited remarkable understanding during each work session. General Lee, Rita's beautiful golden retriever, waited patiently for attention and long walks.

Corwin gratefully acknowledges the contributions of the following reviewers:

Tessie Adams, Reading/Math Instructional Coach
Coteau-Bayou Blue Elementary School
Houma, LA

Jason Fulmer, Program Director
South Carolina Center for Educator Recruitment, Retention,
    and Advancement (CERRA)
North Augusta, SC

Jennifer Harper, Teacher, Grade 4
Cavendish Town Elementary School
Proctorsville, VT

Billie Travis, KDE Educational Recovery Math Specialist
Assigned to The Academy @ Shawnee
Louisville, KY

About the Authors

 **Carolyn Chapman** continues her life's goal as an international educational consultant, author, and teacher. She supports educators in their process of change for today's students. She has taught in a variety of settings from kindergarten to college classrooms. Her interactive, hands-on professional development opportunities focus on challenging the mind to ensure success for learners of all ages. All students *do* learn. Why not take control of that learning by putting excitement and quality in effective learning? Carolyn walks her walk and talks her talk to make a difference in the journey of learning in today's classrooms.

Carolyn authored *If the Shoe Fits . . . How to Develop Multiple Intelligences in the Classroom.* She has coauthored *Multiple Assessments for Multiple Intelligences, Multiple Intelligences Through Centers and Projects, Differentiated Instructional Strategies for Writing in the Content Areas, Differentiated Instructional Strategies: One Size Doesn't Fit All,* and *Test Success in the Brain Compatible Classroom.* Video Journal of Education, Inc., features Carolyn Chapman in *Differentiated Instruction.* Carolyn's company, Creative Learning Connection, Inc., has also produced a CD, *Carolyn Chapman's Making the Shoe Fit,* and training manuals to accompany each of her books. Each of these publications and her trainings demonstrate Carolyn's desire and determination to make an effective impact for educators and students. She may be contacted through the Creative Learning Connection website at www.carolynchapman.com.

Rita King is an international trainer, keynote speaker, consultant, and author. She conducts training sessions for teachers, administrators, and parents. She served as principal and director of the teacher-training program in Middle Tennessee State University's laboratory school. In this capacity, she taught methods courses and conducted demonstration lessons. Educators relate to Rita's background as a teacher and administrator and her experiences in preK–12 classrooms. She has been recognized as an Exemplary Educator by the state of Tennessee.

As an international consultant, Rita conducts training sessions for teachers, administrators, and parents on local, state, and international levels. Her areas of expertise include differentiated strategies for reading, writing, management and assessment, multiple intelligences, practical applications of brain-based research, creating effective learning environments, and strategies for test success.

Rita coauthored *Test Success in the Brain Compatible Classroom*, *Differentiated Instructional Strategies for Reading in the Content Areas*, *Differentiated Instructional Strategies for Writing in the Content Areas*, and *Differentiated Instructional Management*. She also coauthored training manuals to enhance professional development sessions using the reading, writing, management, and assessment books. Multimedia kits are available for use on-site.

Rita's sessions give educators and parents innovative, engaging activities to develop students as self-directed, independent learners. Participants enjoy Rita's practical, easy-to-use strategies, sense of humor, enthusiasm, and genuine desire to foster the love of learning.

Rita may be contacted through the website for King Learning Associates, Inc., at www.kinglearningassociates.com, by phone at (615) 848-8439, or via e-mail at kingrs@bellsouth.net.

ONE TOOL DOESN'T FIT ALL

Introduction

1

In order to make judgments about the status of a student or an entire class at any given point in time, teachers need as much accurate data as possible about an individual student's progress, or the progress of the class as a whole, to determine their next instructional steps.

—Marzano (2010, p. 1)

EFFECTIVE TEACHERS STRATEGICALLY SELECT AN APPROPRIATE assessment tool for each learning situation. In the same way, when planning a construction project, a builder carefully identifies the best preassessment tools including a study of the environment, detailed measurements, an examination of the blueprint, the owner's input and the expertise of everyone involved. During the process, ongoing or periodic inspections are conducted so the subcontractors can make immediate corrections in their special areas. Final inspections are made to reveal needed adjustments.

Like the builder, the teacher chooses the most efficient assessment tools for each purpose. Formative assessment data are gathered before, during, and after learning using a wide variety of instruments. Using various assessments allows students to show what they know in many ways. It takes more than one assessment tool to accurately gauge individual learning.

WHAT IS DIFFERENTIATED ASSESSMENT?

Differentiated assessment is an ongoing process through which teachers gather data before, during, and after instruction using multiple formative and summative tools. Quality assessment is a gauge to navigate the pathways for individual learning. Through interpretation of the assessment data, the teacher identifies each learner's needs and strengths. Each learner can reveal what he or she knows when appropriate assessment tools are used. The teacher analyzes the results and customizes planning to differentiate instruction.

Choosing the Essential Tools

The carpenter uses prior experiences and expertise to assess and analyze the proposed construction project in order to choose the right tools for the procedure, the materials, and the task at hand. The same principles apply to teachers and students on a far more sophisticated and consequential level. Select or design differentiated assessment tools to provide the complete picture of students' needs. Keep in mind that the goal of each assessment experience is to show what the learner needs to know and to improve the individual's ability to master new skills and strategies.

Differentiated assessment tools are needed to gather information about students because each individual is unique in the following ways:

- Knowledge base
- Motivation
- Emotions and desires
- Multiple intelligences

- Prior experiences and background
- Attitude toward the topic or subject
- Learning styles and modalities
- Abilities, interests, and talents

The results are used to strategically tailor instructional plans, provide students with multiple ways to show their learning, keep them on the right track, and accelerate their learning journeys.

Ongoing Assessment

Ongoing assessment provides vital information to improve teaching and learning. The assessment *of* learning is valuable; however, ongoing assessment *for* learning is essential. In traditional classrooms, new material was often taught and evaluated with a test at the end of the unit. During the past few years, ongoing assessment has become integral to the instructional planning process. Educators now realize the value of gathering, interpreting, and applying data before, during, and after learning.

To gain a perspective on the importance of ongoing assessments for learning, *visualize* the following scene: A race car arrives on the track for a major race. Before the race begins, the crew and driver thoroughly check the car's engine, tires, brakes, and safety equipment. During the race, they continue to assess the vehicle combining the data gathered from the electronic instruments with their individual observations and collective expertise. The goal for the team is to maintain the vehicle's maximum performance and speed.

The driver occasionally pulls into the pit so the crew can replace parts, add fuel, change tires, and provide other needed services. If the driver and crew wait until the end of the race to monitor the car's performance, it will be too late to make repairs and adjustments.

Think about a learner's performance in the classroom. Is it reasonable to wait until the end of a unit, a semester, or time period to assess?

Clarifying the Differentiated Assessment Terminology

Many assessment terms used by educators have multiple, debatable meanings. The following definitions and explanations are presented to clarify the terms as they are used in this resource:

Assessment: a judgment or appraisal of the learner's work and specific needs

The direction for immediate and future instruction is based on information gathered with formal or informal procedures.

Assessment Activity: an exercise to actively engage the student, physically and/or cognitively, in the assessment process

The selected activity can be formative or summative and may be designed on varying levels of difficulty to identify the learner's strengths and weaknesses.

Assessment Choices: providing the learner with assessment selection options

This powerful technique immediately differentiates and empowers learners.

For example, ask students to draw a picture or write a paragraph to answer a question.

Assessment Skill: the learner's ability to proficiently use an assessment tool

The student must be able to apply the assessment skill to divulge understanding, knowledge, and ability.

For example, the ability to use a matrix to record information is a skill in using a graphic organizer.

Assessment Strategy: an approach or tactical procedure used to reach a goal

A strategy is an umbrella for activities, skills, or tools. The same strategy can be used in many different activities.

For example, color-coding is a strategy. When red, yellow, and green discs are used to identify knowledge of vocabulary words, it is a color-coding activity.

Assessment Tool: a formal or informal instrument used to identify the student's knowledge level of the standard, skill, or concept

The assessment tools include activities or devices that provide information or data for instructional planning before, during, and after learning. A reflective sentence starter such as "the most important information I learned is ___ " is an example of a metacognitive assessment tool.

Authentic Assessment: a meaningful performance task the learner applies to demonstrate knowledge, skill, strengths, and needs in a realistic authentic manner

For example, simulations, role-plays, exhibits, demonstrations, projects, and portfolios are authentic assessments.

Differentiation: "a philosophy that enables teachers to plan strategically in order to reach the needs of the diverse learners in classrooms today to achieve targeted standards" (Gregory & Chapman, 2007, p. 2)

Differentiated instructional strategies are used to implement this philosophy. Assessment data are the driving force in planning differentiation.

Evaluation: a summative analysis of the learner's abilities and skills at a particular time to make a judgment. Evaluation data are traditionally gathered at the end of a unit of study, a semester, or the year.

Feedback: the teacher's or observer's written or verbal comments related to the learner's work or response

The statements provide constructive suggestions for improvement.

Specific observable praise statements are motivating factors in the feedback process.

Formal Assessment: tools that collect specific, observable information and contribute to a grade

These data may be derived from content knowledge, skills and abilities, or behavior observations. Tests are formal assessment tools.

Formative Assessment: ongoing daily assessment before, during, and after instruction to identify needs and provide continuous feedback

The data gathered can be derived from formal and/or informal assessments. Formative assessment data guide planning for differentiated instruction and provide feedback to enhance the learner's daily academic progress. Ways to gather these data include teacher observations, self-checks, daily work, chapter or unit tests, major exams, and task performances.

Informal Assessment: a process using quick, efficient tools to gather reactions or responses in a casual, yet informative way

These tools usually do not produce a score or grade. Informal assessment tools are easy to design, implement, and analyze.

Some examples are response cards, hand signals, or observations.

Ipsative Assessment: a form of metacognitive self-assessment of a skill by which the learner compares a present performance with a prior performance to set a goal for future improvement

This strategy promotes independence for self-assessment and learning.

For example, in weight training, an individual analyzes the amount of weight lifted and the number of repetitions to set a reasonable future goal.

Students are familiar with this self-assessment principle because they use it in their electronic and computer games to improve their scores. Ipsative assessment removes peer pressure and allows the individual to set personal, attainable goals.

Self-Assessment: a metacognitive process to determine personal strengths and needs

This thinking process leads to ownership of standards, skills, and concepts for the learner to identify activities and strategies to use.

Standards: mandated benchmarks or specific skills identified for mastery in a subject area for specific grade levels

These benchmarks are established at the federal, state, or district levels. Several states are in the process of adopting the national common core standards.

Summative Assessment: evaluation of student work occurring at the end of a unit or period of study

All assessment data are accumulated and analyzed to make instructional decisions and student placements. In the next lesson, this information often becomes a major segment of the formative data.

ANALYZING YOUR VIEW OF DIFFERENTIATED ASSESSMENT

Consider the following statements as a preassessment of your disposition toward differentiated assessment, related teaching experiences, and beliefs in relation to this philosophy (see Figure 1.1).

If you responded with "4" to most or all statements, you are aware of the need for differentiated assessment strategies. Analyze the results and set an improvement goal to incorporate differentiated assessment in your classroom, school, or district.

Figure 1.1 Formative Assessment Self-Analysis				
Rate yourself on the following items—I indicates that you need to incorporate this more often, and 4 indicates you are incorporating this now.				
A. I use formative assessment results to identify a student's need.	I	2	3	4
B. I use informal and formal assessment data to plan instruction.	I	2	3	4
C. I meet the unique strengths and needs of the student.	I	2	3	4
D. I use assessment data to plan differentiated assignments and interventions.	I	2	3	4
E. I believe a student's interest and attitude related to a specific topic directly impacts his or her success with assessment.	I	2	3	4
F. I use a variety of formative assessment tools before, during, and after learning.	I	2	3	4
G. I engage the learners in self-assessment tasks.	I	2	3	4
H. I provide specific assessment feedback in a timely manner.	I	2	3	4

Differentiated assessment identifies a learner's needs and strengths. Use a variety of formal and informal assessment tools to reveal the student's knowledge base, prior experiences, interest level, attitude, and ability in relation to a topic or skill. Analyze the formative assessment results to create personalized plans to meet individual needs.

BUILDING THE TOOLBOX TO "ZAP THE GAPS"

Differentiated instruction and assessment go hand in hand. Marzano (2000) clarifies the goals of assessment and instruction as follows:

- Assessment should focus on students' use of knowledge and complex reasoning rather than their recall of low-level information.
- Instruction must reflect the best of what we know about how learning occurs.

To support this high level of instruction and assessment, the teacher needs a constant stream of assessment data. As the authors, we present formative differentiated assessment strategies and an overflowing box of tools to assess students before, during, and after learning. These tools are designed to help teachers identify students' needs or the holes in learning as they appear, so students can "zap the gaps" and expedite learning.

Differentiation has been pondered, questioned, and researched since teachers first considered the best way to reach individual students. We predict that differentiated instruction and differentiated assessment will become common practices, as research provides more details about how the brain learns and how assessment guides and supports planning.

> Formative assessment is a planned process in which assessment-elicited evidence of students' status is used by teachers to adjust their ongoing instructional procedures or by students to adjust their current learning tactics.
>
> —Popham (2010, p. 138)

Practical applications of the research are found in various strategies and activities presented throughout this book. More research is embedded in the methods, models, and approaches to differentiated assessment.

We hope educators use these formative and summative differentiated assessment tools to customize learning experiences. We have designed or selected numerous strategies, activities, and ideas so teachers can strategically adapt them to plan interventions and empower their students.

ASSESSMENT IN THE AGE OF ACCOUNTABILITY

How does formative, differentiated assessment help schools meet accountability standards? Educators use this approach to customize planning. Differentiated instruction and formative assessment address educational standards with novel, intriguing strategies and skills in the diverse ways students learn.

The goal of formative assessment is to use the most appropriate tool for the learner to demonstrate knowledge and skills. As students are presented with assessment activities, they are provided with opportunities to become reflective, self-assessing, internally motivated learners, capable of reaching their learning potentials. Formative, differentiated assessment provides an ongoing loop of assessment data to guide decisions related to instructional planning. Differentiation assists individual students in succeeding with standards and in making yearly progress.

National Common Core Standards

The Common Core State Standards are the result of an initiative from the National Governor's Education Center for Best Practices and the Council of State School Officers. These standards focus on core understandings and procedures for student mastery, providing expectations for each grade level. The goal is to ensure student progress while preparing each learner for success in college and in the workforce.

The Common Core State Standards . . .

- Are aligned with college and work expectations
- Include rigorous content and application of knowledge through higher order thinking skills
- Build upon strengths and lessons of current state standards
- Prepare learners to succeed in our global economy and society
- Are evidence- and research-based

The use of the Common Core State Standards and assessments increases the capacity for states to share and compare data in a meaningful manner.

Race to the Top

Race to the Top provides states with monetary incentives for educational reform. It is funded by the American Recovery and Reinvestment Act announced in July 2009. The major goal is to reform American education and ensure that every child has access to an excellent education. It is designed to provide all stakeholders with data and information needed to continuously improve teaching and learning.

The Race to the Top criteria related to assessment include developing and implementing common standards and high-quality assessments. State data are analyzed and applied to improve instruction. One category places science, technology, engineering, and math (STEM) as a priority in the instructional program. States have to qualify with an intense application to receive the funds. After approval, many strenuous guidelines must be followed and implemented.

Response to Intervention

Response to Intervention (RTI) was written into the Individuals with Disabilities Education Act in 2004. It is designed as a three-tiered framework for instruction, assessments, and interventions to meet the needs of struggling students. The overall goal of

RTI is to target the needs of individual learners so they will not be assigned to special placements outside the classroom. This is a general education initiative, but it can be applied in special education programs.

The three levels of intervention are as follows:

- Tier I: Specific individual weaknesses and needs are identified through formative assessments and general screening. Decisions are based on gathered data. Differentiated instruction is implemented to target the identified needs of the learner.
- Tier II: More intensive screenings with targeted interventions are provided for students who did not respond to the approaches in Tier I. Progress monitoring occurs more often in this level with research-based instruction.
- Tier III: Specific, intensive interventions are provided through special education services to students who did not improve through targeted instruction provided in Tier II. Adapted inclusion models are used to serve the learner's needs.

The Impact of High-Stakes Testing

The term *high-stakes testing* refers to the major impact the results have on students, teachers, schools, communities, states, or the nation. Here are a few examples of test score impact on stakeholders:

Students

- Test results are used to make pass–fail decisions.
- Graduation depends on test success.
- Participation in sports is denied to individuals with low grades.
- Acceptance or rejection in special classes depends on the scores.
- Students with low scores often become discouraged and drop out of school.

Teachers

- In some states, salary incentives and sanctions are based on improved scores.
- Colleagues feel pressured as scores are publicized and compared.
- Less time is available to create meaningful, hands-on activities for students to experience the joy of learning.
- Mandated improvement programs for higher test results bring stress and anxiety to teachers who have low-performing students.

Schools

- Test scores of schools in the district and state are compared.
- Sanctions on low-achieving schools result in reduced federal funding.
- Specific programs are mandated to improve test scores.
- Interpretation of testing data is the basis for planning differentiated instruction.

Community

- Parents avoid purchasing homes or leave neighborhoods in areas with low-performing schools.
- Students are moved to private schools. This causes less public school funding.
- Businesses move into areas with high-performing schools.

State

- Businesses and families select their location in states with high-performing test scores.
- The scores are ranked from the highest- to lowest-performing districts and reported in the media.
- Low-performing schools are identified and monitored by the state.

Nation

- The results are ranked according to each state's performance.
- Federal funding is disseminated to the states based on the scores.
- States are held accountable for improvement.
- The composite scores for the nation are compared and ranked with other countries.

Assessment as a Prerequisite

Differentiated assessment is a prerequisite to curriculum planning and instruction. Formative assessment activities and strategies provide data to use in planning decisions for differentiation. This addresses the many ways students vary in their experiences and knowledge base. Consider the three-group scenario presented in the following.

Group One needs the background information expanded to provide a stronger foundation related to the topic. Interventions are used to fill in the gaps in the background knowledge.

Group Two possesses the knowledge and background needed to begin the lesson. This group's preassessment data reveals that they are ready for the grade level information.

Group Three is ready to accelerate beyond the basics, expand their knowledge, and explore or investigate new areas related to the topic. The assessment data reveal that they have the proper background and are reviewing the mastered grade-level material being introduced.

When a skill or a piece of factual information is taught, the student may use it correctly following the lesson. Remember that true mastery is evident when the learner uses the skill automatically after several days have passed.

Use assessment data to design a rich, rigorous, differentiated curriculum to meet the needs of individual learners on their varying knowledge levels.

The Benefits of Differentiated Assessment Strategies

Students and teachers benefit from differentiated assessment because data gathered from various sources provide a metaphoric mosaic of each student's readiness for learning specific skills or topics. The mosaic artwork is complete when each piece is in place to complete a design. Some mosaics are created from a multitude of small pieces, while others are composed of a few large puzzle pieces. Compile various pieces of assessment data to produce a complete picture of a student's unique needs.

One standard may require detailed assessment data to complete the whole picture. In another case, a quick observation of students may provide adequate assessment data to use in planning because students need only one or two pieces of the puzzle. If the standard is composed of complex thinking processes, it may require multiple assessments to complete a total, in-depth view of the student. Educators and the learner benefit when they work together to make all pieces fit.

In a differentiated classroom, provide opportunities for all students to use higher-order thinking skills. Too often, students who excel are the only learners presented with these tasks. Those who have difficulty learning are too often given basic, rote assignments and assessments. All students benefit need to be challenged with essential skills, questions, processes, and ideas to learn within their personal levels of understanding.

An assessment may indicate the need for explicit instruction, review, or reteaching. It may point to the necessity of presenting the information or skill with a new or different approach. Individuals benefit when the teacher intervenes with assistance as soon as a need is recognized (see Figure 1.2). It is important for students to know the teacher is continually monitoring their strengths and needs to help them grow cognitively and affectively.

Figure 1.2   Cognitive and Affective Benefits of Ongoing Differentiated Assessment

Cognitive Benefits

- Uses assessment data to intervene and avoid gaps in learning
- Reduces failure
- Challenges within the learner's level of success
- Increases time on task
- Builds on the learner's knowledge base, experiences, and ability
- Accelerates learning

Affective Benefits

- Encourages and empowers learners
- Provides security
- Supports risk taking
- Uses mistakes as learning opportunities
- Creates bonds
- Reduces frustration
- Develops confidence
- Generates self-motivation

WHAT IS THE TEACHER'S ROLE IN DIFFERENTIATED ASSESSMENT?

According to the *New Oxford American Dictionary,* the word *assessment* means "appraisal" ("Assessment," 2010). It is derived from the Latin word *assidere*, which means "to sit beside." In an ideal situation, the teacher sits beside the student during the assessment activity to provide support and immediate feedback. The learner receives instruction in each skill as a need evolves. It is physically impossible to sit beside each student during an assessment. However, it is possible for a student to feel that the teacher is his or her personal coach and cheerleader. All learners need to know the teacher is there as a guide to provide assistance, praise, encouragement, and high expectations.

Teachers are required to follow mandated state standards, benchmarks, essential questions, or indicators. In most cases, they have the autonomy to choose the resources, techniques, and appropriate times to teach the required skills. When assessment experiences are orchestrated with intriguing tools and strategies, opportunities are created to open doors to learning.

The teacher's multidimensional task is to differentiate assessment experiences using the most effective approach of the following:

Content	Resources	Tools	Formats
Tasks	Strategies	Feedback Techniques	Performances

The teacher uses results from a variety of assessment experiences to determine students' learning levels. Students have opportunities to demonstrate that they have the appropriate background, know the information, and are ready for the next step.

Assessment data are used to determine if learners need more work on particular skills or if they are ready to move on to new skills. These critical, decision-making assessment experiences are discussed throughout this book.

Taking the Initial Steps

Take Small Steps Into Differentiated Assessment

When using this resource independently, proceed incrementally. It contains a vast treasure trove of ongoing assessment ideas. When approaching differentiated instruction and assessment for the first time, choose one or two of your favorite

> While the evaluation process depends on assessment, assessment is only the first step in the evaluation process. Data, by itself—without observational components and interpretation— has no meaningful place in instruction or informed teaching. You can't make a value judgment about test scores; they are merely raw data. It's the interpretation of that data which brings one to the evaluation level.
>
> —Routman (2000)

strategies for implementation. For example, start by giving students choices. Begin on a limited basis, and expand the use of the tools as you grow more comfortable

Figure 1.3 Implementation Phases for Differentiated Formative Assessment

Phase One	Phase Two	Phase Three
Use few assessment tools before the learning.	Use some assessment tools before each learning segment	Use appropriate preassessment tools one to three weeks before for planning instruction.
Use observation and quick check quizzes during the learning.	Adjust assignments based on preassessment data.	Develop a large formative assessment toolbox.
Provide end of study assessments.	Use informal and formal assessment tools to gauge learning.	Use data effectively to plan for individual needs.
Understand that there are many different ways to learn.	Provide Choice with activities for students to show what they know.	Provide self-assessment opportunities.
Plan varied ways to teach materials.	Use teacher-focused and student-focused activities.	Assess before, during and after learning using informal and formal tools.
Use little, if any, self-assessment.	Establish centers, stations or learning zones.	Use surveys and have informal conversations routinely to know the students and use the data in personalized planning.
Provide few independent and small group assignments.	Plan instruction with Flexible Grouping using total groups, students working alone, partners and small groups (TAPS)	Use flexible grouping strategies moving students as needed.
Adults grade student's papers.	Use knowledge base to group learners.	Level activities for centers and independent assignments.
Teach students and standards with the most effective resources and materials.	Survey students to identify their knowledge base and interests.	Use portfolios as grading support the grade.
Use surveys and inventories to know the students.	Provide Choice activities for performance assessments.	Create grades by combining scores from grade level and knowledge level assessments.
Create a positive assessment climate.	Use computer programs to assess on the learner's level of success.	Use assessment data to plan adjustable assignments.
Monitor learning through questioning and discussion.	Vary graphic organizer designs for assessment.	Assign individual contracts and agendas based on data.
Group randomly, by interests or ability.	Use projects with an emphasis on the learners' thinking processes.	
Engage learners in assessment activities.	Provide interventions to fill in learning gaps.	

Where are you in implementing Differentiated Formative Assessment?

Phase One ←→ Phase Two Phase Three →

with them. For example, on a unit test, allow students to choose how they want to show their understanding of the water cycle. The options may include writing a description, drawing the process, or labeling the major transitions and phases. Gradually expand the students' assessment choices as you use this powerful strategy. Next, add self-talk or cubing options. Have the student work with each strategy until it feels natural. As the benefits are reaped, dip back into this resource to expand your repertoire.

Use Differentiated Assessment
Tools as Job-Embedded Experiences

Staff developers and administrators will find that the differentiated assessment activities and strategies may be presented to teachers as job-embedded experiences. This involves on-site demonstrations to model careful selection of the tools or approaches to meet the diverse needs of an individual or group of students. To accomplish this rewarding task, grade-level teams or colleague partners may select a book section or chapter and present specific assessment tools through exhibits and role-playing. In follow-up activities, include an analysis and a discussion of practical ways to adapt the identified tools.

Figure 1.3, Implementation Phases for Formative Differentiated Assessment, is designed as a self-analysis and improvement tool for teachers. Check each item in all columns, if it is currently implemented in the classroom. Phase III items reflect expertise in using formative differentiated assessment. Items not marked in Phases I and II indicate areas for improvement. Use the form with individuals or teams for professional development.

OPENING THE TOOLBOX

Design adjustable assignments by using the appropriate assessment tools to identify the learner's knowledge base and prior experiences related to a standard, topic, or skill. Use the information gathered to guide instruction, so each student begins on his or her level of understanding and grows during the learning process. Identify the student's entry point for instruction using differentiated assessment data to provide the most productive learning opportunities.

Practical applications of the research presented here are found in the various strategies and activities presented throughout the book. More research is embedded in the methods, models, and approaches to differentiated assessment.

We hope educators use these tools to personalize assessment experiences. We designed or selected the numerous strategies, activities, and ideas so you can strategically adapt and use each one as a differentiated assessment tool since . . .

One tool doesn't fit all.

BRINGING RESEARCH AND BEST PRACTICES TO DIFFERENTIATED FORMATIVE ASSESSMENT 2

Essential Question: How can brain research be used to enhance and customize assessment experiences to make them personally meaningful for diverse learners?

The strategies, activities, and suggestions in this resource are based on recent brain research and effective learning and assessment techniques. This chapter presents an overview of theories, effective practices, and current research that influence and guide our work with differentiated assessment. Use these ideas to apply the research to the data-gathering process.

PROCESSING INFORMATION AND MEMORY

It is important for educators to understand how basic brain functions relate to information processing to improve each learner's assessment experiences. In *How the Brain Learns*, David Sousa (2006) explains that during each experience and learning activity, the brain filters incoming information. The sensory register analyzes it and acts as a guard, to turn it away or to admit it, based in part on past experience with related input. If the information is determined to be nonthreatening or insignificant, it may be discarded. If deemed to be important, valuable, or meaningful, the information enters working memory. Keep in mind that the student, not the teacher, determines the importance, value, or need. Even for the student, this is usually an unconscious process.

Mel Levine (2002), a pediatrician and learning expert, states that a student may have difficulty deciding what is important. If a learner does not possess an effective filtering system, the brain takes in worthless or useless information. Another student may receive important information but be unable to focus on specific segments of it. It is important to explicitly model how to identify valuable information. If the student focuses, or pays attention, the brain transfers information into working memory.

Students need to know how to develop their ability to retain information. This, too, must be explicitly taught in daily activities. For instance, learners need to know the role of focused attention in activating the brain and opening the gateways to memory. They need to be familiar with strategies that connect prior experiences, attach meaning, and prepare information for long-term storage. This is accomplished by working with the information, organizing the facts or ideas, and creating retrieval cues. When students have opportunities to thoroughly process information in working memory, they are likely to store it in ways that make retrieval easy and automatic. A learner's success with each assessment experience depends on his or her memory skills and ability to retrieve the requested information.

WHY STUDENTS FORGET AND WHY THEY REMEMBER

Following an assessment, teachers often say, "I just taught this information. I can't believe they didn't remember it!" Figure 2.1 presents practical interpretations of these factors and provides some possible solutions for each one.

Figure 2.1 Chapman and King's Memory Obstacles Chart		
Memory Obstacles	*Description*	*Prescriptions*
Lapse of Memory	Information is forgotten over time. Facts and skills are not remembered. *"If you do not use it you lose it!"*	Use facts in stations for practice. Create sponge activities. Use mnemonic devices. Link old and new information. Spiral or revisit important information. Use facts and skills in a game format.
Inattentive	The mind is on something else. Attention is not focused. Physical discomfort is evident. *"In another world!"*	Consciously design focus activities for the learner. Use high-interest materials. Provide routine practice sessions to ensure ownership. Redirect with novelty. Change the task. Share information with a partner. Move to a different position. Assign as a helper or assistant with the task.
Lack of Retrieval Cues	Information is known but it cannot be expressed. *"It is on the tip of my tongue."*	Make links and connections with new and old material. Ask the learner to relate it to his or her world. Teach and model memory cues. Reteach and review. Give time for retrieval. Remove distractions.

Memory Obstacles	Description	Prescriptions
Distorted Facts and Skills	Previous information was learned incorrectly. *"Bamboozled."*	Reteach to clarify. Provide learner time to clear misunderstandings. Discuss with peers for clarity. Research facts. Correct errors immediately. Provide time for students to work with new information.
Personal Agenda Obstacles	Feelings, biases, beliefs, and emotions hinder learning. *"That is what I believe."*	Respect differences and expose to information and skills in a new way. Engage in one-on-one discussions. Provide time for Socratic discussions. Organize debate sessions. Create a factual platform.
An Established Mind-Set	Ideas are cemented in the mind and cannot be forgotten. Information is learned one way, so it is difficult to learn a new approach. *"Doing it my way!"*	Identify correct ideas, and use them to bridge it to new information. Provide time to make links and connections. Create techniques for easy transfer of information. Honor correct information.
No Background Knowledge	There is little or no experience with the task or information. Lost! *"I am out in left field."*	Assess to identify the learner's knowledge base. Provide interventions to fill gaps. Design focus activities. Use high-interest materials. Use novelty. Provide routine practice sessions to ensure ownership.
Fact Confusion	There is trouble distinguishing the difference of the look, sound, or meaning of terms. *"Too much to handle!"*	Separate introduction of confusing terms. Introduce and learn one segment. Introduce the other segment in another time period. Teach using different modalities. Post visuals to illustrate the differences.
External Interruptions	Outside noises or actions interfere and grab attention. A loud disturbance, intercom announcement, or inappropriate behavior pulls learners off task. *"What was that?"*	Avoid disturbing interruptions in your control. Change the task so the learner does not need to concentrate during noisy interruptions. Deal quietly and privately with behavioral issues to avoid interrupting student work and thinking.

ASSIST THE BRAIN IN MEMORY PROCESSING

Working memory is the thinking or processing stage of learning. To help students transfer information to long-term memory, present strategies that give the brain opportunities to work with new information. Use the following guidelines to present new terms, topics, and skills. Create examples similar to the suggested categories in the following list to assist learners as they mentally manipulate and process new information. Use the following statements and questions with an important term from your content that needs to be stored in the learner's long-term memory.

Make Personal Connections

Discuss ways students observe or apply _____ in their daily activities. This provides personal connections and associations with the term and makes students more conscious of the benefit and frequency of its use in their present and future lives.

Choose one or two topics from the following list to introduce and explain to students how _____ is experienced in their daily activities:

After school, a student uses _____ when he or she . . .

At school, a student experiences _____ when he or she . . .

In the workplace, _____ is used when . . .

After an introduction, challenge students to identify additional ways they use *the term* in their activities in and out of school. Compile the responses to create a class list on a chart or poster.

Project the Value of the New Information

- This information on _____ will be valuable to you when . . .
- When you know how to use _____ tools automatically, you will be able to . . .

Organize and Categorize the Facts, Thoughts, and Ideas

- List various ways you use _____ in daily activities.
- Write steps to the _____ activity in sequential order.

Make Connections to Prior Knowledge and Experiences

- How have you used _____ in the past?
- How has _____ guided you to improve a skill?

Analyze the Component

- Examine each step of the _____ activity.
- Explain each component of the _____ tool in your own words.

Summarize the Component

- Explain all steps used with the _____ tool in a nutshell or brief paragraph.
- What are the essential features of the _____ strategy?

Evaluate the Component

- How is _____ valuable in the work of someone you know?
- How useful will _____ be to you throughout your school years?

Apply Memory Strategies to Create Retrieval Cues

- Design a mnemonic strategy to record and remember _____ facts.
- Create a song, rap, jingle, or poem to remember the terms related to _____.

A student's success with each standard and skill depends on his or her ability to process, record, and apply information in the required format. Provide experiences that incorporate these ideas to optimize learning and enhance memory of important vocabulary.

Transfer

Effective teachers plan instruction for automatic transfer of information and skills to similar or new situations. The ability to use new knowledge is the learner's key to success. Assessments reveal the student's ability to apply or transfer knowledge.

A major goal of instruction is to show the learner how to apply facts, skills, or ideas in different ways after some time has elapsed. Students need to understand that information must transfer to have value. Students are more likely to transfer learned information, skills, and ideas to assessment activities when you . . .

- Create meaningful experiences.
- Use terms that are easy to understand and apply.
- Provide examples related to their world.
- Intervene as needed with productive feedback.
- Make understanding the focus of teaching and learning.
- Apply new learning to other academic areas and their lives.
- Use a variety of differentiated assessment tools for simulations, demonstrations, and performances.
- Showcase their knowledge of facts, skills, or ideas in their own, unique personal ways.

Novelty

Novelty is anything new, different, or unique that captures the mind's attention. According to David Sousa (2006), the brain is alert and constantly scanning the environment for stimuli and responding to it. Take advantage of this phenomenon to focus and maintain the student's attention. Use novel strategies, such as the following examples, to build anticipation and create curiosity to enhance instruction and assessment experiences:

- Model and practice with intriguing memory strategies and retrieval cues.
- Employ flexible grouping scenarios.
- Implement a variety of formats, materials, and tools.
- Introduce information with hooks to grab attention.
- Use intriguing problem-solving experiences to stretch the mind.

Automaticity

Automaticity is the student's ability to easily access and immediately apply information stored in memory. When students quickly and correctly apply information as needed, true automaticity is demonstrated. An example of automaticity is evident in first-draft writing. If students use correct punctuation as they answer open-ended questions on a written test, complete a first-draft writing assignment, or write a note to a friend, punctuation mastery is evident.

If you ask students to demonstrate the same knowledge the following week, they may not recall the information. If this occurs, the skill or information was learned for the moment, not for long-term application or lifetime use. True mastery is demonstrated when students transfer knowledge correctly and automatically in various situations after several days or weeks have elapsed. Establish automaticity as the goal for mastery of each assessed skill and strategy.

DEVELOP INTELLIGENT BEHAVIORS FOR ASSESSMENT

In his book, *The School as a Home for the Mind*, Art Costa (2008) presents a list of characteristics that reflect intelligent behaviors. Students who consistently receive high assessment scores usually exhibit these behaviors.

Foster Intelligent Behaviors During Assessment Experiences

It is important to incorporate intelligent behaviors in daily lessons and routines to empower learners during assessments. In the following section, the authors select six intelligent behaviors and apply them to assessment. Explanations for the behaviors are presented with suggestions and ideas for use with students. Use the sayings on banners and posters or in raps and jingles to reinforce the behaviors.

Persistence

Persistence is an individual's desire to continue efforts to complete a task. Create assessments to provide opportunities for success. Teach each student within his or her zone of proximal development. This zone is the level where the student is capable of learning with some assistance (Vygotsky, 1978). In this learning stage, the student does not feel too bored or too challenged. Reward a student's efforts with specific, genuine praise.

> Winners never quit.

Share examples of persistence in the lives of famous heroes, role models, and champions such as the following:

Abraham Lincoln	Michael Jordan	Phil Mickelson
Helen Keller	Mary Kay	Oprah Winfrey

Quality

Emphasize and praise the *quality*, not the quantity or amount of the learner's work. Show students how to do the following:

- Identify quality or what is important, such as setting obtainable priorities and goals
- Analyze materials and distinguish between the least and most valuable items
- Practice selective abandonment

Demonstrate the following examples of self-talk as praise statements for quality work habits:

> Be the best that you can be!

- Wow! I did a great job on that problem.
- Yes! I completed my assignment correctly.
- I am proud of myself because I . . .

Decrease Impulsivity

The impulsive learner often acts without thinking, becoming careless with assessment activities. This student needs to see the value of thinking through personal actions and decisions. Remind the learner that spontaneity is an advantage in many situations, but impulsivity often becomes detrimental during assessments.

> Haste makes waste!
>
> —John Heywood

Share the fable "The Tortoise and the Hare." Discuss the lesson reflected in the turtle's steadfast determination and consistent movement toward goals. Identify and model the stick-with-it steps students use to process, retrieve, review, and check information during assessments.

Metacognition

Teach the value of metacognition, or "thinking about thinking." Model self-talk strategies the learner can use to activate metacognition. Remember it takes time to think.

The following are examples of learner self-talk to prompt metacognitive thinking during assessment:

- How do I solve this problem?
- Can I repeat the directions?
- Am I following the correct sequence or procedure?
- I'll check my work to see if I followed the rules.

I think about my thinking!

- Is there a better way to complete this task?
- What steps did I use to complete the problem?

Striving for Accuracy and Precision

Teach skills that eliminate incorrect responses. Model steps to check personal work. For example, after a student completes an addition problem by adding from top to bottom, demonstrate how to check it by adding from bottom to top.

A stitch in time saves nine.

Emphasize the value of reading directions thoroughly before beginning tasks in daily work and assessments. Adapt the following activity to all subjects and grade levels.

Activity: Following Directions

In the following activity, it becomes clear to learners that they need to read and follow the directions. When students "read all directions before beginning," they see that number 5 tells them not to complete the first four directions. The only items to complete are numbers 6 and 7.

Read all directions before beginning the following activity. Work until you hear a signal to stop.

1. Draw a square.
2. Divide the square into four smaller squares.
3. Draw a diagonal line in each small square to create two right triangles.
4. Draw a star in each right triangle.
5. Do not complete the previous directions for numbers 1 through 4.
6. Make a list of your favorite books, movies, foods, or television shows until the teacher gives the signal to stop.
7. Stand up. Pat yourself on the back, and say "yes!" if you read all directions first.

Note: This activity illustrates the value of reading all directions before beginning an activity. Students "get" this message and enjoy similar activities.

Applying Past Knowledge to New Situations

Refer to the student's past and current knowledge to make meaningful connections to the new skill or strategy. Find out as much as you can about his or her experiences, attitude, and background in relation to a topic. These factors have a major impact on learning. Create opportunities for the student to recall past experiences. Explain many ways to activate prior knowledge and build on personal experiences to make mental connections to new facts or ideas.

Examples: Applying Past Knowledge to New Situations

- Draw a cartoon to illustrate your knowledge.
- Write about it.
- Discuss with a partner how your knowledge or experiences relate to the new information.
- Create a rap to describe how your past experiences can be used with the new skill.
- Preassess prior experiences using surveys, inventories, and questions.
- Role play related past experience.
- Use the following self-reflective questions.
  - Where have I heard about this skill or strategy before?
  - How have I used this information in the past?
  - How can I use what I know to work with the new information?

AUTHENTIC ASSESSMENT

Authentic assessment presents activities that give learners opportunities to use information or skills in realistic situations (Campbell, 2000). This alternative to formal and standardized testing is recognized as providing the best evidence of learning because students must show that they can recall and apply the information, concept, or skill in different ways. The teacher designs authentic assessment activities and experiences by engaging students in tasks that simulate realistic experiences. Model how to use each tool so students understand and know how to apply it. Students are more likely to store information when they have opportunities to use it in personal, meaningful ways.

Teachers and those who support instruction need to know when and how to use all assessment tools available to them. In his book, *Student-Involved Classroom Assessment,* R. J. Stiggins (2001) advocates a balanced perspective with respect to the use of assessment methods. Stiggins suggests the use of selected student-response formats, essay assessment, performance assessment, and personal communication with students. He asserts that none of these alternatives is inherently more or less powerful or appropriate than other approaches. Each can serve well when developed and implemented in the right context by informed users. Figure 2.2 identifies some distinguishing characteristics of traditional and authentic approaches to assessment.

Grant Wiggins (1999), an expert in the field of educational assessment, affirms that authentic assessment should be a "direct examination of student performance on worthy intellectual tasks."

Figure 2.2 Views of Traditional and Authentic Assessment		
Traditional Assessment		
Easy to administer	Use a checking key	Quick, easy grading
Uses low-level thinking	Requires short answer	
Reflects recall ability	Learns information for the test	
Authentic Assessment		
Applies to real-life situations	Hands-on activities	Shows what is learned
Uses multiple skills in a task	Demonstrations of ability to apply information	
Is ongoing for days, weeks, or throughout a study	Reflects growth in a skill or ability	

According to Wiggins, authentic assessment does the following:

- Offers students a variety of tasks using acquired knowledge and real-life skills, such as collaboration, research, writing, revising, and discussing
- Assists in discovering whether students can create valid answers, performances, or products
- Standardizes criteria to achieve validity and reliability for scoring projects
- Guides students to rehearse for authentic roles in adult life

PERFORMANCE FEEDBACK

Performance feedback accelerates learning and empowers a student. This authentic analysis has been emphasized in the results of numerous studies as a technique to enhance student achievement. Feedback accelerates learning. According to Marzano, Pickering, and Pollock (2001), when corrective feedback is presented in a timely manner, students have great opportunities to improve. Differentiated assessment is designed to provide students with the specific feedback and guidance they need to be successful in daily activities and assignments.

> Appropriate, ongoing assessment keeps the learner on track in the learning journey.
>
> —Chapman and King (2008)

SUMMARY

The latest research emphasizes the value of using differentiated assessment to assist learners as their needs occur in daily activities. Individuals receive prompt interventions with specific, corrective feedback as they work. This avoids the pitfalls of failure as students learn to monitor their work and take personal control of learning.

CREATING A CLIMATE FOR FORMATIVE ASSESSMENT 3

Essential Question: How is the classroom environment designed to create a positive learning climate during each differentiated assessment experience?

In an effective classroom, learners view each assessment activity as a way to highlight their strengths and needs so they can improve, extend, and celebrate learning. In other words, each formative assessment is approached and perceived as a productive experience.

THE AFFECTIVE DOMAIN AND ASSESSMENT

When a positive climate is evident in a classroom, each person knows he or she belongs to a learning community. This culture is reflected in daily activities, assignments, and interactions. In this environment, students know they are valued team members.

The affective domain of teaching and learning includes all areas that influence students' emotions, including their mind-sets, levels of interest, and motivations. Negative feelings create barriers to success, so it is imperative for the teacher to maintain a positive, comfortable, and inviting assessment environment.

Students' perceptions of the classroom climate are affected by the teacher's presence and personal interactions. Voice tone, high expectations, energy, enthusiasm, and genuine interest are key elements in the assessment atmosphere. Continually monitor the affective aspects of the environment

> We believe everyone benefits when tests are viewed as celebrations of the brain's phenomenal abilities, not dreaded events.
>
> —Chapman & King (2009c)

to assure student success. For example, it is important to promptly recognize the telltale signs of confusion or frustration. Reteaching, intervention, and clarification remove these barriers to learning.

One incident can instantaneously change a student's attitude from positive to negative, so monitor individual feelings. Be consciously aware of how words and body language are perceived, especially when identifying learner errors in assessment feedback. When a student's negative feeling is detected, reestablish a positive attitude for optimal learning.

The affective assessment climate is reflected in personal desire to grow in understanding. This is evident when someone exclaims "I got it!" "Let me show you how I figured it out a different way," or "Help me, I don't understand this at all." In the last example, the student is seeking assistance from classmates or the teacher. In this atmosphere, the student knows help is available.

EMOTIONS

An emotionally safe environment plays a major role in the brain's level of functioning during assessment activities. If an individual has unpleasant memories or experiences with a topic, subject, teacher, or classroom design, these internal feelings interfere with learning and assessment. If a student has pleasant, stimulating learning adventures, the mind becomes an open vessel for new learning. This individual is eager to show what he or she knows. Remember this attitude may change quickly if new experiences become negative or unchallenging.

> Emotion is our biological thermostat and is thus central to cognition and educational practice.
>
> —Sylwester (2000)

Pay close attention to the emotions tied to the assessment. Negative emotions often block or interfere with mental pathways that lead to memory. If the student is emotionally and academically prepared for an assessment experience, he or she is more able to link, retrieve, and apply previously learned information and skills.

EMOTIONAL INTELLIGENCE

The classic work of Daniel Goleman (2006) on emotional intelligence applies to differentiated assessment. Goleman describes the intellect as working "in concert" with the emotions. The gamut of emotions is evident in assessment activities: anxiety, frustration, dread, disappointment, embarrassment, pride, pleasure, and exhilaration.

Figure 3.1 contains the emotional intelligences as defined by Goleman. Share the indicator examples with students. Strategically plan learning and assessment activities to foster these characteristics.

Risk Taking as Emotional Bravery

Explain to students that risk-taking experiences can lead to uncomfortable, unknown territory or knowledge. They need to know why each risk requires emotional bravery. Inform students that their effort may result in errors or mistakes. The risk may leave them open to negative comments or bring success and result in celebrations. Remind everyone of the good feelings produced by bravery. Model the risk-taking strategies needed for success with assessment tasks. For example, demonstrate the value of an educated or "smart" guess as an action reflecting individual persistence. Make students feel eager to apply more thinking to find the best answer so they put

Figure 3.1 Formative Assessment and the Emotional Intelligences

Goleman's Emotional Intelligences	Relevant Indicators	Application to Formative Assessment
Self-Awareness	• Understands feelings • Knows strengths and needs • Applies positive thinking to boost self-confidence • Monitors and assesses personal needs and success	• Complete surveys and inventories. • Assign journal responses. • Provide self-check opportunities. • Use self-assessment tools. • Promote self-praise. • Celebrate accomplishments.
Self-Regulation	• Delays gratification to pursue goals • Works to complete personal and academic tasks • Possesses the ability to recover from setbacks • Continually uses self-assessment for improvement	• Administer time tests. • Give agenda assignments. • Teach time on task skills. • Incorporate skills for resilience. • Require assignments to be turned in on time. • Teach independence. • Provide assignments with check points and self-assessment opportunities.
Motivation	• Shows initiative • Has an innate desire to overcome weaknesses and improve • Keeps trying after failure • Strives to succeed in each assessment experience	• Know each student's strengths and weaknesses. • Tie personal interests and hobbies to learning. • Exhibit high expectations. • Give specific praise. • Administer assessment tool in a timely manner for learner success.
Empathy	• Feels what others are feeling • Respects diverse views of other individuals • Is loyal and supportive • Is willing to assist others with personal and academic needs	• Understand how the learner feels. • Teach students to honor peer weaknesses and strengths. • Teach praise statement to use as a conferencing tool. • Establish a community of caring learners.
Social Skills	• Is a valued team member • Uses effective verbal and nonverbal communication • Gets along with others • Learns during partner and group work	• Provide opportunities for respectful collaboration. • Share appropriate statements to use during small-group work and discussions. • Explicitly model and practice social behaviors. • Establish a culture for learning.

forth this effort in future activities. Each risk deserves praise. Teach self-talk techniques for risk taking. Here are a few examples:

I give myself a pat on the back because I tried!

I am proud of myself because I always do my best.

Remember, self-confidence and the desire to improve are prerequisites for taking risks. Maintain a classroom atmosphere that promotes and praises individual risk taking as a valuable assessment skill.

SELF-EFFICACY

Self-efficacy is the student's belief in "self" and in the ability to succeed. This feeling plays a major role in the learner's efforts during assessment experiences. When the student believes it is possible to reach the expected level of mastery, he or she will try. However, if the student feels inadequate, little or no effort will be exhibited.

Donna Tileston (2004) refers to self-efficacy as the silver bullet—"one of the most powerful ways that we can impact the brain toward motivation" (p. 83). The silver bullet has two parts. They are (1) teaching the vocabulary of the standardized test and (2) using context for teaching. Engage the students in strategies and activities that make assessment vocabulary user-friendly. Empower learners with a clear understanding of new information using their prior knowledge and by making connections to real-life situations.

One of the best ways to develop self-efficacy is to design assessment tasks on the student's success level. When the assessment is too easy, students often work carelessly. When it is too difficult, they become frustrated.

Each comment and gesture by the teacher reflects his or her feelings and attitudes related to assessment. The teacher's body language and verbal innuendos have a significant impact on the way learners respond to assessments. These feelings leave impressions that endure for a lifetime.

Post slogans similar to the following to promote self-efficacy:

I believe in ME!

I will, I will, I will ZAP the GAPS!

I am a success because I do my best!

Negative Teacher Messages

We have to complete this assessment. We don't have a choice.

I don't want to do this either.

We can _____ as soon as we finish.

Positive Teacher Messages

Show how much you've learned!

I am anxious to see your answers!

Show your best work!

Post and discuss this phrase for daily viewing.

Attitude Is Altitude!

This mind-set has to be present for the teacher and learners to reach their potentials. Learning takes place when the material is presented in a way that "hooks" students and keeps them focused. To develop a positive attitude about learning, students must believe they need the information and that it is relevant to their lives.

Each lesson has the potential to turn a student on or off to future learning experiences. As information enters the brain, a student unconsciously but automatically analyzes it. As illustrated in Figure 3.2, the student's emotions produce thoughts that automatically open or close the gateways to memory.

Figure 3.2 Watch What You Say!

Examine the following sample statements that may close or open gateways to memory:

Closing the Mind	*Opening the Mind*
I can't use this information.	I can use this information when I _____.
This does not apply to me.	I remember _____from _____.
This is not for me.	This is exactly what I need to know.
I don't like this!	Wow! This is going to be interesting.

MOTIVATION FOR ASSESSMENT

A great teaching challenge is to maintain a student's desire to learn. Teachers often say a student is capable but not interested in completing assessment tasks. Is it more likely that he or she may be unchallenged? Lack of engagement often occurs when there is repetition in assessment activities. When the student perceives the activity as monotonous or boring, his or her mind wanders and focuses on unrelated thoughts or daily events. In this mental state, the learner misses vital or intriguing directions and information. The individual does not automatically "turn on the switch" to examine his or her own learning or to engage in an activity because the preoccupied mind does not hear the signal that an upcoming event is meaningful or of personal interest. This state of unawareness affects a learner's cognitive growth. The teacher holds the keys to motivation.

Pleasure, derived from effort and success, is a strong and natural motivator. Plan assessment activities on the student's success level. When a learner's efforts are rewarded, he or she has the desire to engage in the activity again. Plan and maintain positive experiences in all aspects of assessment to generate pleasurable, intrinsic motivation.

Balance the Learner's Level of Concern

The learner's desire to succeed plays an important role in the amount of mental and physical energy the individual exerts to succeed in a task. When motivational levels are too low, a student may exhibit an "I don't care" attitude. Previous failures, boredom, peer pressure, and an unchallenged mind contribute to this state. Plan many successful experiences to raise the level of concern and develop an internal desire to succeed.

When expectations are too high, the student may experience stress and anxiety. This may be evident when parents and teachers place too much pressure on the learner. This may be self-induced and result in a fear of failure. These feelings often create an anxious state that interferes with thinking.

Be aware of the student's level of concern, and strategically raise or lower the level of anxiety so his or her mental activity is dedicated to the assessment task. The level of concern can fluctuate with topics, the settings, teachers, or situations in the learner's personal life.

Use a continuum similar to Figure 3.3 to assess the attitude and feelings of an individual toward an assessment task. Number 1 on the scale represents the student who has "no desire" to work. This student's refusal to complete the assessment demonstrates a low level of concern. On the opposite end of the scale, number 8 represents the student who demonstrates "great desire," or a high level of concern. This is exhibited in the learner's strong drive to correctly complete the task.

Success breeds success. Students who experience success enjoy and receive personal satisfaction. They strive to succeed again to create the same feelings. Keep this in mind as assessment tools, strategies, and activities are selected to balance the student's productive levels of concern.

"Withitness"

Teachers and students view "withitness" differently, but, by either definition, each connotation contributes to teacher success. The term *withitness* was coined by Kounin (1970) to describe the teacher's awareness of learners' behaviors at all times.

Figure 3.3   The Engagement–Disengagement Spectrum of Feelings and Responses

Feelings	Possible Observed Reactions
No desire to engage in assessment	
1. I am not going to do this.	Does not do it
2. I'd rather do anything else.	Does something else
3. I do not want to do this.	Exhibits a negative attitude
4. I'll just do the easy parts.	Completes a few items
5. I will do enough to stay out of trouble.	Tasks are incomplete
6. I have to complete this because it is required.	Does enough to get by
7. I understand, and I am going to do this.	Completes it to the best of his or her ability
8. I am excited about doing my very best on this work.	Does the best work possible
Great desire to engage in assessment	

He describes teachers who exhibit this attribute as being "tuned in" to their students' needs. They may seem to have eyes in the back of their heads and know what each student is doing, thinking, or feeling. These teachers display an ability to perceive problem behaviors and stop them before they escalate. These special educators appear to have a natural intuition that patiently advises and guides students with general expertise and wisdom.

Learners perceive with-it teachers as keeping current with the latest trends and fads. These teachers stay abreast of students' hobbies, interests, and other free-time activities. This awareness can be used as a bonding technique. Give assessment tools and activities titles with words, phrases, or names from students' favorite songs, movies, sitcoms, musical groups, sports, or fashion styles. Learners recognize and respond to teachers who exhibit withitness because it validates the youth culture when information is bridged to their lives.

Become so familiar with a student's hobbies and interests that it is easy to refer to these outside activities in informal conversations when an opportunity presents itself. Provide an area for individuals to spotlight their interests and accomplishments with photos, notes, or newspaper clippings. Knowledge of the student's personal, free-time activities and interests often provides valuable data that create avenues for motivation, instruction, and assessment.

Student-to-Student Behavior Expectations

Students need to know that unacceptable behaviors toward each other are not tolerated during assessments. Adapt Figure 3.4 to your learners. Encourage students to add ideas to the chart. Use skits to demonstrate unacceptable behaviors, and follow up with scenarios illustrating valued behaviors. Culminate the activities with in-depth discussions of the behavior expectations.

Reinforce expectations whenever the opportunity arises. Use specific feedback, as in the following examples:

You made a mistake by _____, so you need to _____.

I like the way you _____. This time, add _____.

Figure 3.4 Student-to-Student Behavior Expectations	
Unacceptable Behaviors	*Valued Behaviors*
Put-Downs/Sarcasm • Is that the best you can do? • That doesn't make sense. • You didn't think through that answer.	Encouraging Comments • Way to go! • Good try! • Good thinking.
Negative Gestures • Frowning • Gasping in awe • Dropping the shoulders • Slumping in disappointment	Positive Gestures • Smiles • Thumbs-up • Nods of the head • High fives

Celebrate Assessment Success

Create an exciting atmosphere to celebrate learning by planning special events related to assessment. For example, choose a unique, enticing name to build anticipation and curiosity for the assessment activity. When an assessment day is announced, use a catchy title for the day. Students are more likely to remember the assessment if they hear the teacher say . . .

Don't forget, on Marvelous Monday we will show what we know about _____ in our Squaring Off activity.

Examples: Days of the Week

Marvelous Monday:	Squaring Off
Terrific Tuesday:	Partner Pairing
Wacky Wednesday:	Standards, Stations, and Centers of Choice
Thinking Thursday:	Brainy Text Talk
Fantastic Friday:	Presentations and Celebrations

Promote Positive Feelings for Assessment

Find ways to generate anticipation and excitement before, during, and after assessment activities. Give learners opportunities to make suggestions and plan celebrations as in the following examples:

- Give each other a high five and a good luck wish!
- Share a pat on the back.
- Make celebration banners, posters, or balloons from brightly colored paper.
- Post messages to promote success, such as "Soar With Success," "Fly High!" or "Give It Your Best!"

> If you want to build a ship, don't herd people together to collect wood and don't assign them tasks and work but rather, teach them to long for the endless immensity of the sea.
>
> —Antoine de Saint-Exupery

Design each assessment strategy to entice learners to give their best efforts. Provide opportunities for learners to review their results so they are encouraged to keep making attempts that produce progress and growth. Select strategies that motivate students as they engage in assessment activities. Motivated individuals are more apt to use their best efforts and thinking skills.

THE PHYSICAL ENVIRONMENT

The physical environment has a positive or negative effect on students' assessment experiences. It consists of the type of seats, the furniture arrangement, visuals, lighting, air quality, and temperature. Included are the objects in the immediate vicinity and the peripherals, or visible surroundings. Everything within the physical setting plays a major role in the learning climate and affects the student-environment fit.

Activity: Yuk Spots/Bright Spots—Scavenger Hunt

This activity is designed for teachers and students to identify physical aspects of the classroom or work areas that need to be improved or maintained. Places or things to improve are *Yuk Spots*. The areas to maintain are *Bright Spots*.

Yuk Spots Directions

Step A

1. Create teams, and ask each group to select a team name.

2. Have each team identify a captain and a recorder.
   - Captain's role: Bring the team together and lead discussions.
   - Recorder's role: Record findings for the team during the activity.

3. Send the teams on a scavenger hunt tour of the school including halls, classrooms, work areas, or special areas. If needed, set time limits.

4. Ask each team to record their findings for Yuk Spots on the chart provided (see Figure 3.5).

5. Identify the Yuk Spots throughout the school that need to be improved to enhance the environment using Figure 3.5 to record the discoveries. When a team member finds something that needs to be repaired or improved in the school's physical setting, the recorder lists it as a Yuk Spot in the first column under "What Is It?" and then completes the "Where Is It?" column to identify the location.

6. When the scavenger hunt is complete, each team returns to share the findings.

Step B

1. Compile a list of the Yuk Spot areas.

2. Prioritize this list from the quick-fix item to the most difficult to determine short-term or long-term action plans. If an identified Yuk Spot can be fixed within a brief period of time with a minimum amount of labor and effort, this area is corrected first.

3. The teams write suggestions for improvement on each item.

4. Establish a plan of action to take care of these immediate short-term goal needs.

5. If it is costly, takes an extended amount of time, or requires an extensive workforce, it is recorded as a long-term goal. Place these needs on a timeline with an implementation plan for each item. Think about including needed materials, costs, individuals responsible for each task, and the completion date.

Note: Talk with the teams about how some Yuk Spots must be addressed and changes approved by administrators or staff members. These areas can be identified with suggested action steps. The list may be sent to the principal or individuals responsible to request improvements and volunteer assistance.

Figure 3.5   Yuk Spots Chart

What Is It?	Where Is It?	Suggested Improvements	Action Plans

Team Name _____

Captain's Name _____

Recorder's Name _____

Team Members _____

_____

Date of Tour_____

Bright Spots Directions

1. Form teams to go on the school tour or scavenger hunt to identify the Bright Spots throughout the school that enhance the environment. These are the existing places and spaces that brighten, enhance, and support a positive learning climate. Establish a time to return to the commons area.

2. Each team records their comments and ideas related to each identified Bright Spot on the chart in Figure 3.6. As each Bright Spot is discovered on the tour, the recorder lists each one in the column "What Is It?" and gives the location in the column "Where Is It?"

3. Return to the commons area.

4. Each team completes the remaining columns with brainstormed responses.

Figure 3.6   Bright Spot Findings

What Is It?	Where Is It?	Why Do We Need to Keep It?	What Changes Are Needed?

Team Name _____

Captain's Name _____

Recorder's Name _____

Team Members _____

_____

Date of Tour_____

SETTING CLIMATE GOALS

After assessing the climate, look at specific areas of need. Set goals and establish a plan for improvement (see Figures 3.7 and 3.8). Remember, short-term goals are easier to reach, so address these plans first. When everyone sees immediate improvements in the learning environment, feelings of accomplishment are exhilarating. Add goals as needed to the chart.

Figure 3.7   Climate Goals: An Implementation Grid

Goal	Procedures/Actions for Implementation	Progress Notes
1.		
2.		
3.		

Figure 3.8   Teacher Assessment of the Classroom Environment

The environment will strongly benefit from the teacher's evaluation, too. Aspects for scrutiny should include the physical environment but extend to deeper realms of learner support as well. Adapt the following chart to analyze the learning environment for assessment experiences. Check the appropriate boxes.

Teacher _____   Class _____   Date _____

Classroom Environment	Rarely	Sometimes	Often	Most of the Time
Students are . . .				
1. Given time to think.				
2. Encouraged to take risks.				
3. Becoming self-directed learners.				
4. Comfortable when asking and answering questions.				
5. Learning from mistakes and accomplishments.				
6. Aware that learning is acquired by building on prior experiences and background knowledge.				
7. Given opportunities to learn from others and to work alone.				
8. Provided self-assessment opportunities.				
9. Guided to see mistakes as learning experiences.				
10. Treated with respect.				
11. Given specific praise.				
12. Honored for efforts, strengths, and talents.				
13. Valued as members of the learning community.				
The physical arrangement of the classroom . . .				
1. Promotes learning.				
2. Permits flexible grouping for assessment.				
3. Is customized to meet the learner's assessment needs.				
4. Is conducive to productive experiences.				
5. Is inviting and comfortable.				
6. Accommodates personal needs.				
7. Honors diversity.				

Classroom Environment	Rarely	Sometimes	Often	Most of the Time
The classroom visuals ...				
1. Are samples of student work.				
2. Reflect student learning.				
3. Showcase the learner's strengths and growth.				
4. Are novel, effective learning tools.				
5. Are displayed at students' eye levels.				
6. Contain assessment reminders and tips.				
7. Correlate with the current topic or unit of study.				
8. Are student centered.				
9. Celebrate assessment success.				

Variation: Ask students to complete the checklist to see how they view the classroom's climate. Combine the teacher and student responses to improve the classroom's learning culture.

Follow-Up Discussion Probes

- What areas need improvement?
- How will I improve this area?
- What do I need to make the improvements?

A productive climate has a significant effect on students' attitudes toward immediate and future experiences related to assessment. In this environment, students realize that everyone has areas to improve. They learn the value of using effective strategies to identify their needs, so they become comfortable saying to themselves and others, "I don't understand this part." This statement indicates that the students are striving to "zap the gaps" in their learning.

Teachers must continually monitor the classroom to find ways to optimize the assessment environment to meet each student's cognitive and affective needs. The general climate has a direct impact on the learner's success.

Think about the learning climate in which most assessments are administered.

> When someone is taught the joy of learning, it becomes a lifelong process that never stops, a process that creates a logical individual. That is the challenge and joy of teaching.
>
> —Marva Collins

Did *positive testing environment* come to mind? To some, this phrase qualifies as an oxymoron because the words *positive* and *testing* are usually incompatible. An air of negativity often surrounds most assessment scenes escalating frustration, especially for struggling learners. Because the brain functions best in a stimulating and psychologically safe environment, negativity must be eliminated.

Present each assessment experience in a relaxed atmosphere where high expectations are evident without creating undue stress and anxiety. When assessment data are interpreted and shared to guide curriculum decisions and instruction, students and teachers are aware of individual needs. This keeps learners involved in a challenging, rewarding environment, creating feelings of growth and accomplishment.

SUMMARY

The climate has a major influence on the student's motivation and success with the assessment experiences. In a productive classroom, all aspects of the environment promote learning during instruction and assessment activities.

Establish a positive learning climate for students to automatically assess and monitor their skills and seek assistance because they have the desire to improve. Maintain this environment to empower learners and develop their personal navigation systems for success.

KNOWING THE LEARNER 4

The potential possibilities of a child are the most intriguing and stimulating thing in all creation.

—Ray L. Wilbur

Essential Question: How does knowledge of the learner's learning styles, intelligences, personalities, knowledge base, and interests assist in the selection and use of differentiated assessment strategies?

Effective teachers know it is worth their time to gather as much information as possible about each student and not assume anything. This chapter provides useful strategies and ideas for gathering valuable data on each learner. It provides tips to gather information through formal and informal assessment tools. With the results, teachers can diagnose problems or situations to strategically plan for the diverse needs of individual learners.

INFORMATION GATHERING

Teachers gain knowledge of each student by noting correct, incorrect, appropriate, or inappropriate responses. It is important to have an expanded collection of tools to obtain data to identify the student's level of understanding, interests, intervention needs, and individual learning styles.

It takes time to think, assess, and analyze gathered information. Step back, interpret, and make the right instructional decisions. Avoid jumping to the wrong conclusion by making incorrect assumptions and generalizations or by taking action too quickly. When a student performs below his or her potential, the vigilant teacher recognizes *when* this is happening, identifies the student's performance level, and analyzes *why* it is occurring. Adjustments are made to the plans to meet the learner's performance level.

The goal in education is for all individuals to learn as much as they can to be productive citizens and maintain personal success in today's world. As educators, we know all students can learn. We also know that most students can learn more than they are learning. Think about the way students are captivated for hours by an electronic game. This occurs because the activity is for their minds. The bottom line is people learn about things and techniques of interest to them. Meaningful knowledge and experiences are usually stored in long-term memory. After each learning experience, ask yourself, "Was the activity mentally engaging for the individual learners? Do the assessment results indicate who truly understands this information? Which students need more strategically planned interventions? What do I plan next?" See Figure 4.1.

A student is more likely to learn information and be able to apply it when the assessment experience includes the following:

- High-interest activities
- Accommodations to meet the individual's needs
- Presentation within the learner's window of opportunity
- An appropriate time frame
- A significant or practical purpose
- A valuable use of time
- Intriguing activities to generate commitment to the task
- Stimulating approaches to create the desire to improve
- Celebration of successes

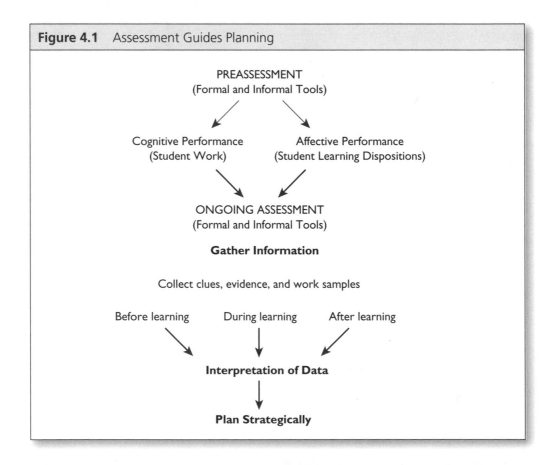

Figure 4.1 Assessment Guides Planning

PREASSESSMENT
(Formal and Informal Tools)

Cognitive Performance
(Student Work)

Affective Performance
(Student Learning Dispositions)

ONGOING ASSESSMENT
(Formal and Informal Tools)

Gather Information

Collect clues, evidence, and work samples

Before learning   During learning   After learning

Interpretation of Data

Plan Strategically

Observing the Learner

Teachers can become practiced at considering the following questions as they observe students:

- What is the individual's knowledge base at the beginning of the unit of study?
  - What does the learner know?
  - What is the student's attitude and feelings toward the new learning?
  - How can the student's prior knowledge be assessed?

- What does the student need to learn next?
  - What are the identified gaps in the student's learning?
  - How can I address the prioritized needs?
  - What is the most effective experience this individual needs to learn and retain the information?

- What are the observable behaviors?
  - Is the behavior causing a problem with the learning?
  - How can the behavior be modified or corrected?
  - How will the learner demonstrate competence?

- How will I teach the information?
  - How will I use the formative assessment data to guide instruction?
  - How will I use the individuals' learning styles, modalities, and intelligences to teach the information?
  - How will I engage learners in meaningful lessons?
  - Which strategies and activities will engage the high-end learners in meaningful, challenging activities?
  - What are the appropriate interventions to "zap the gaps"?

- How will I check for understanding?
  - Which assessment tools do I need to use with this student during and after the learning?
  - How will I provide the feedback?
  - How can I engage the student in self-assessment experiences?
  - What is the best assessment for the learner to demonstrate knowledge and skill mastery?

- How will the new information be retained or crystallized?
  - When will I revisit or link this information in another learning situation for review?
  - When and how will I provide opportunities for making links and connections in real-world situations?
  - How will the learner demonstrate ownership of the information or skill?

GARDNER'S MULTIPLE INTELLIGENCE THEORY

Howard Gardner (2011) named "intelligences," or abilities, that are possessed by every individual. This theory is an effective planning tool to use to meet the diverse needs of learners. It works because the students' academic needs can be addressed with strategies and activities that target their strongest intelligences.

Eight of the intelligences are selected for practical application in the classroom. Gardner's theory proves that intelligence is not fixed and an intelligence can be developed over a lifetime. Eight intelligences identified are shown in Figure 4.2.

Figure 4.2 Dr. Howard Gardner's Multiple Intelligences		
Language-Related Intelligences	*Object-Related Intelligences*	*Person-Related Intelligences*
Verbal/Linguistic Musical/Rhythmic	Logical/Mathematical Visual/Spatial Bodily/Kinesthetic Naturalist	Intrapersonal Interpersonal

Everyone has areas of strengths and weaknesses. Students perform best when they use their strongest intelligences. Throughout life, as individuals explore and accumulate knowledge, their intelligences strengthen and grow. They can also improve their strengths and weaker intelligences. Sharing this theory with students gives them new ways to view their current areas for growth.

Repertoire of Assessment Tools

Teachers often plan instructional activities and assessments in their own areas of strength. For example, teachers with strong visual/spatial intelligence tend to employ art and design techniques in lessons. An individual's areas of strength may not match the teacher's area of strength. For example, struggling math students may have strengths in the area of music. They are able to learn math facts using raps, jingles, and rhymes. If teachers are not musically inclined, they must leave their comfort zones and find musical approaches to reach these learners. The students' favorite ways to learn are avenues to optimal assessment results. We strongly recommend that teachers create a collection or list of assessment tools correlated with all intelligences so they will be ready to select and implement them as needed.

Research shows a number of ways to view learners' intelligences, thinking, and learning styles. Analyze the complete profile of a student and its effect on how he or she approaches, engages, and demonstrates learning. Remember to use this information to provide lessons and assessments that allow each student to achieve success.

The eight intelligences listed in Figure 4.3 include the signs or names individuals might wear if they are strong in a particular intelligence. The chart also lists assessment tools and career choices for each intelligence. It is important to differentiate assessment experiences by choosing assessment tools and activities that incorporate varied intelligences. Whenever possible, allow students to show their learning in ways that feel natural and comfortable.

Figure 4.3	Meet the Intelligences		
Intelligence	*My Sign*	*Assessment Tools and Activities*	*Career Choices*
Verbal/ Linguistic	*The Communicating You!* *The Comprehending You!* *The Wordy You!* Includes Listening Reading Speaking Writing Linking ideas	Essays Audio recordings Reports Speeches Debates Interviews Research projects Quizzes or tests Logs, journals, diaries Questions and answers Observations/findings Oral reports Explanations Written assignments Jokes Exhibits Posters Critical factual writing Creative writing Writing or telling Various genres	Journalist Teacher Announcer Actor Storyteller Comedian Speaker Author
Musical/ Rhythmic	*The Dancing You!* *The Musical You!* *The Rhythmic You!* Includes Tonal patterns Musical talents Identification of sounds	Musical patterns Songs Raps Poetry Rhythmic patterns and beats Jingles Cheers Background sounds and noises Musical compositions Recordings Chants Tonal patterns Jump rope rhymes Show tunes Limericks	Musician Dancer Sound technician Composer Band director Poet Conductor

(Continued)

Figure 4.3 (Continued)

Intelligence	My Sign	Assessment Tools and Activities	Career Choices

Logical/ Mathematical	*The Gadget You!*
	The Pattern-Seeking You!
	The Analyzing You!
	Includes
	   Numbers
	   Technology
	   Problem solving
	   Logical thinking
		Sequential steps
		Fact analysis
		Research
		Logic problems
		Attribute groupings
		Problem-solving techniques
		Outlines
		Reasons and rationales
		Predictions
		Rubrics
		Demonstrations
		Calculations
		Statistics/data
		Research projects
		Graphic organizers
		Labels
		Categorizing activities
		Manipulatives
		Gadgets/calculators
		Formulas
		Thinking games
		Patterns
		Process explanations
		Timelines
			Inventor
			Programmer
			Analyst
			Technician
			Accountant
			Engineer
			Broker
			Banker
			Economist
			Accountant
			Technician
			Programmer

Visual/Spatial	*The Creative You!*
	The Artistic You!
	The Designer You!
	Includes
	   Art media
	   Visualization
	   Spatial relationships
		Color, lines, and shapes
		Creative designs
		Sculptures
		Visualizations
		Imagination
		Graphic organizers
		Visuals
		Art media
		Displays
		Posters
		Charts
		Brochures
		Pictures
		Illustrations
		Cartoons and caricatures
		Color-coding
			Artist
			Designer
			Builder
			Fashion coordinator
			Makeup artist
			Architect
			Engineer
			Choreographer

Intelligence	My Sign	Assessment Tools and Activities	Career Choices

Bodily/ Kinesthetic	*The Athlete You!*
	The Tactile You!
	Includes
	    Fine gross motor skills
	    Sport participation
	    Performance
		Manipulatives
		Mimes
		Inventions
		Sports participation
		Demonstrations using physical movement
		Exercises
		Human representations
		Hands-on experiences
		Simulations/Role-playing
		Field trips
		Demonstrations
		Dramatic interpretations
		Movement routines
			Actor
			Athlete
			Seamstress
			Lab technician
			Surgeon
			Dentist

Naturalist	*The Scientific You!*
	The Survivor You!
	The Outdoor You!
	Includes
	    Science
	    Environmental issues
	    Saving the planet
	    All areas of nature
		Demonstrations of environmental sensitivity
		Awareness of surroundings
		Appreciation of nature
		Recognitions of science and nature
		Classifications
		Survival skills
		Creations of environmental scenes
		Nature collections
		Problem solving in environmental situations
		Research of nature topics
		Real-life situations
			Environmentalist
			Farmer
			Oceanographer
			Astronaut
			Zoologist
			Scientist
			Explorer
			Archeologist
			Conservationist
			Forest ranger

Intrapersonal	*The Independent You!*
	The Goal-Setting You!
	The Metacognitive You!
	Includes
	    Personal decision-making
	    Working alone
	    Self-efficacy
		Private conferences
		Knowledge of self
		Surveys and inventories
		Journal entries
		Logs and diaries
		Tests/exams
		Self-studies and contracts
		Personal choices
		Metacognitive engagement
		Independent work
		Portfolios
		Personal reflections
			Computer geek
			Program analyst
			Accountant
			Journalist
			Counselor
			Technician

(Continued)

Figure 4.3 (Continued)			
Intelligence	My Sign	Assessment Tools and Activities	Career Choices

Interpersonal	The Social Butterfly You!
	The Team Player You!
	The Cooperative You!
	Includes
	    Joining groups
	    Conforming
	    Making group decisions
		Communications with others
		Teamwork
		Questions
		Demonstrations of intuitiveness
		Partner reports
		Reenactments
		Cooperative learning
		Text talk
		Participation in literary circles
		Human graphs
			Teacher
			Receptionist
			Talk show host
			Counselor
			Psychologist
			Minister
			Politician

Use the following key points to implement the multiple intelligence theory in differentiated assessment experiences:

> It is not "how" smart you are, but how you are smart.
>
> —Howard Gardner (2011)

- Everyone is born with a genetically formed brain that is unique.
- Knowledge and experiences mold and change the brain.
- Everyone has at least eight intelligences.
- People have three or four areas of strength among their intelligences.
- Weaker intelligences can be strengthened. People learn and remember more information when participating in activities that engage their strongest intelligences.

Activity: Tear Into Your Intelligences

The following activity gives teachers and students an opportunity to conduct a self-assessment of their intelligences. It identifies three or four of an individual's strongest intelligences and at least one or two intelligences that may need to be strengthened.

1. Choose eight distinctly different colors of construction paper.

2. List the eight intelligences on a chart. Color-code the intelligences by placing a small piece of the colored construction paper beside each one. Examples: Verbal/Linguistic = orange; Naturalist = green.

3. Cut the construction paper into equal strips so everyone has one strip to match each intelligence color.

4. Label the top of each strip with the intelligence that matches the color on the chart.

Use a key similar to the following to abbreviate the title of each intelligence:

Verbal/Linguistic = V/L   Musical/Rhythmic = M/R

Logical/Mathematical = L/M   Visual/Spatial = V/S

Bodily/Kinesthetic = B/K   Naturalist = N

Intrapersonal = Intra   Interpersonal = Inter

5. Instruct students to keep the full length of each intelligence strip that matches their three or four strongest intelligences.

6. Show them how to tear off the bottom of each intelligence strip to match their weaker intelligences. For example, the corresponding strip will be very short if the student perceives the intelligence as being extremely weak.

7. Tear off the bottom of the remaining strips so the length represents the strength or weakness of each intelligence area.

Teacher Reflection Sample

How do your strongest intelligences impact the learner and your choice of assessment tools (see Figure 4.4)?

Figure 4.4   Activity: Intelligences and You

Place a star beside three or four of your strongest intelligences and a check mark beside two or three of your weakest intelligences:

_____ Verbal/Linguistic   _____ Bodily/Kinesthetic

_____ Musical/Rhythmic   _____ Naturalist

_____ Logical/Mathematical   _____ Intrapersonal

_____ Visual/Spatial   _____ Interpersonal

My three or four strongest intelligences are _____, _____, _____, and _____.

How do I learn best?

How do I like to show what I know?

The intelligences that I need to strengthen are ....

How do the results of the activity reflect the way I teach?

EXPLORING GOLEMAN AND STERNBERG

In Chapter 2, we examined the domain that Goleman (2006) describes for emotional intelligence. In addition, Robert Sternberg (1997), author of the triarchic theory of "successful intelligence," identifies the cognitive aspects of creativity, analysis, and practicality as profiles for success. Form groups with a representative from each intelligence to create productive cooperative teams. Teachers can introduce these attributes and give students guidance to foster metacognitive skills. Figure 4.5 presents the views of Goleman and Sternberg.

Figure 4.5 More Experts' Views	
Goleman's Emotional Intelligences	*Sternberg's Triarchical Theory*

Self-Awareness
  • Understands feelings
  • Has self-confidence
 	
Self-Regulation
  • Maintains focus
  • Delays gratification
  • Demonstrates independence
  • Completes tasks
 	
Motivation
  • Has initiative
  • Has the desire to learn and improve
  • Exhibits resilience
 	
Empathy
  • Feels what others are feeling
  • Understands the views of others
  • Gives support to others
 	
Social Skills
  • Cooperates
  • Is a good team member
  • Works well in groups to reach common goals
	Practical
	  • Gives the meaning
	  • Determines the usefulness
	  • Uses an experience in a personal way
	
	Analytical
	  • Digs for details
	  • Gives specific details, attributes, reasons, and characteristics
	  • Researches and solves
	  • Breaks it into smaller steps or parts for understanding
	
	Creative
	  • Designs a "new way"
	  • Uses innovative thinking and approaches
	  • Brainstorms many solutions

THROUGH ANIMALS' EYES

Use animal characteristics to assist in identifying the way an individual student approaches and works on tasks, such as a problem to solve or an assessment piece. Think about the best learning situations and strategies for students who exhibit the characteristics as described in Figure 4.6.

TRUE COLORS THROUGH OBJECTS

The following chart investigates various aspects of the learner to enhance differentiated instruction and assessment. Teachers find it easy to discuss a student's personality and emotions, but they seldom use personality factors to customize learning strategies and activities. Use Figures 4.7, 4.9, and 4.10 to engage students in analyzing the way they learn.

Figure 4.6   Through Animal Eyes

Animal	Characteristics and Personality Traits
Chameleon	• Conforms to the group • Wants to please • Blends with the environment
Tiger	• Lines up attack technique • Leaps with focus • Plans the approach • Carries through the task quickly
Turtle	• Is slow in taking risks • Takes cautious steps to reach a goal • Thinks before moving forward • Maintains focus • Uses self-pacing • Is methodical
Owl	• Is a metacognitive thinker • Looks for details • Is wise • Views all sides of an issues • Thinks before acting
Parrot	• Is a follower • Mimics sound and behavior • Needs role models • Is dependent on others • Needs to be occupied • Is a loyal partner • Needs routines and procedures • Needs repetitive practice
Beaver	• Keeps busy • Stays on task • Gets the job done • Structures work • Is a hardworking team member • Views each task as a personal mission • Eagerly approaches complex tasks
Butterfly	• Is active • Has unpredictable moves • Is productive • Celebrates success • Develops at its own pace • Has unique characteristics
Dog	• Is a loyal empathizer • Seeks attention • Needs feedback and praise • Strives to please • Needs routines and directions

(Continued)

Figure 4.6	(Continued)
Animal	Characteristics and Personality Traits
Bat	• Exhibits unconventional academic and personal habits • Has a unique view • Is a nonconformist • Uses novel work patterns • Has special needs

Figure 4.7   True Colors Through Objects

Color
  • Green—The Organizer
Object
  • Daily planner
Traits
  • Organizes
  • Needs structure
  • Is a list maker
  • Thinks sequentially
	Color
	  • Gold—The Researcher
	Object
	  • Magnifying glass
	Traits
	  • Analyzes
	  • Is a data seeker
	  • Brainstorms
	  • Looks for details

Color
  • Blue—The Friend
Object
  • Teddy bear
Traits
  • Needs a safe environment
  • Respects others
  • Is a team player
  • Is social
	Color
	  • Orange—The Adventurer
	Object
	  • Spinning top
	Traits
	  • Is flexible
	  • Enjoys multitasking
	  • Is spontaneous
	  • Needs choices

ASSESSING STUDENTS' PERCEPTUAL STYLES

Caine and Caine (2005) provide the following descriptors of learning styles. Use the list with students to identify their sensory styles (see Figure 4.8). Adapt the indicators and suggested activities in discussions and tasks to reveal commonalities and differences. Use the assessment results to tailor instructional plans.

Challenge students to design a chart that reflects their learning styles and characteristics. Provide examples of various descriptors and indicators. Ask them to replace the hat descriptors by choosing a general category and indicators from games, shoes, musical instruments, or sports. This activity (Figure 4.9) engages the learners in constructing a self-assessment tool (also see Figure 4.10). Figure 4.11 is a guide to explore personality characteristics and identify the learner's preferred way to demonstrate knowledge.

Figure 4.8   Perceptual Styles

Descriptors	Indicators	Suggested Assessment Activities
Adventurer *(Multisensory)*	• Enjoys change and variety • Anticipates the future • Prefers to guess • Is spontaneous • Is creative • Engages in multitasking	Manipulatives Projects Demonstrations Games Station assignments Field trips
Director *(Sense of Sound Dominates)*	• Values words and sound • Searches for facts • Is impatient with detail • Enjoys directing • Leads without consideration of others	Oral reports Interviews Research PowerPoint presentations Webinars Blogs
Evaluator *(Sense of Vision Dominates)*	• Values organization • Is concerned with the view of others • Enjoys planning • Lacks ability to adjust to unexpected events	Sequencing tasks Outlining information Graphic organizers Fact gathering Web searches Agendas
Nurturer *(Emotions Dominate)*	• Values relationships and feelings • Enjoys helping others • Is dedicated to causes • Desires to please	Cooperative learning Partner learning Socratic circles Learning communities Reciprocal teaching Teamwork

Source: Adapted from Caine and Caine (2005, pp. 227–229).

Figure 4.9   Activity: Getting to Know Me—An Object View

Give students the following activity to explore understanding of themselves as learners.

1. Number the four objects in the order that they symbolize you.

   a. _____ Daily planner   b. _____ Magnifying glass   c. _____ Teddy bear   d. _____ Spinning top

2. List the objects in the order that they symbolize you, and complete each sentence.

   a. I am *most* like a _____ because I _____.
   b. I am also like a _____ because I _____.
   c. I am *least* like a _____ because I _____.

Figure 4.10   An Object View of Learners

Daily Planner

 This student is organized and thrives on routine. He or she follows the rules, works purposefully, pays attention to detail, and approaches tasks systematically. This learner performs best when assessment activities provide the following:

- Clear, precise directions and procedures
- Routines
- A purpose with clear expectations
- Organization
- Accessible materials
- Established time allotments
- Facts and details
- Guided practice
- Sequential activities
- Agendas

Personalized assessment tools for the daily planner include the following:

- Checklists
- Likert scales
- Rubrics
- True/false statements
- Fill in the blanks
- Multiple-choice tests
- Sequencing activities

Magnifying Glass

 This student enjoys discovering answers by responding to an essential question, researching, analyzing, proving, and problem solving. This learner performs best when assessment activities provide the following:

- Details
- Research
- Exploration and analysis
- In-depth study
- Probing or "why" questions
- Reports using data
- Detailed directions
- Opportunities to ask questions

Personalized assessment tools for the magnifying glass include the following:

- Facts and supporting details
- Open-ended essays
- Forums
- Debates
- Discussions
- Research and data gathering
- Projects

Teddy Bear

 This student is a communicator and collaborator who needs a comfortable environment and frequent encouragement. He or she enjoys working with a partner or small group. This learner performs best when assessment activities provide the following:

- Opportunities to work with other people
- Approval
- Open lines for communication
- A comfortable environment
- Feelings of safety
- A sense of belonging
- Appreciation for sensitivity
- Genuine expressions of encouragement
- Opportunities to receive personal feedback

Personalized assessment tools for the teddy bear include the following:

- Inventories
- Surveys
- Partner and small-group learning
- Conferences
- Personal feedback
- Cooperative tasks

Spinning Top

This student enjoys a variety of creative choices thriving on fast-paced, hands-on challenges. The spinning top is an eager, active participant who enjoys creating projects or games. This learner performs best when assessment activities provide the following:

- Choices
- Variety
- Creativity
- Practical applications

- Fun, stimulating activities
- Hands-on, multitask assignments
- Fast-paced, exciting challenges
- Celebrations

Personalized assessment tools for the spinning top include the following:

- Demonstrations
- Simulations
- Experiments
- Projects
- Choice boards

- Role-playing
- Brain teasers
- Games
- Complex challenging tasks
- Performance

Figure 4.11   Four Ways of Knowing and Showing

Another perspective on how students differ in the ways they prefer to show learning comes from the work of Carl Jung and Isabel Briggs Myers. The following chart is adapted from the work of Silver, Strong, and Perini (2000). Use the ideas as examples to assess students in the ways they prefer to demonstrate their knowledge.

Self-Expressive	Mastery	Understanding	Interpersonal
Needs to explain in his or her own way	*Needs to report, memorize, practice, and exhibit*	*Present or apply knowledge*	*Working empathetically, showing feelings and attitudes*
Assessment Tasks • Interpret • Create • Design • Act out • Demonstrate • Draw • Give point of view	Assessment Tasks • Present it • Practice and demonstrate • Complete a deductive problem • Respond to short-answer tests • Show it	Assessment Tasks • Compare and contrast • Explore • Use an inquiry model • Make discoveries • Use facts to form opinions • Research • Analyze • Critique	Assessment Tasks • Relate personally • Simulate actions and events • Engage in cooperative events • Be a team member • Participate in celebrations

Source: Adapted from Silver et al. (2000).

ENGAGING LEARNER VIEWS

The following activities and strategies are a toolbox of ideas to use in any differentiated classroom.

1. Provide Journal Time

Assign journal writing in various formats so students openly share what they know through their thoughts, questions, and concerns before, during, and after learning. Avoid repeating the same journal entry formats and genres. Present a variety of journal adventures for students to show their thinking processes, attitudes, learning, and needs in novel, intriguing ways.

2. Listen, Talk, Learn, and Know

Engage students in productive conversations about their personal lives as well as school matters. Ask for suggestions, and be open to responses. Be aware that some comments are private and others are open to discussion. Be sensitive to the appropriate times for each type of discussion.

3. Survey Work Preferences

Survey students to identify their work preferences. Discover where each learner works and concentrates best. Students do their most productive work when their preferences are accommodated. Analyze the results, and discover how to assess the learners.

Use the following instrument (Figure 4.12) to accommodate the student's working preferences whenever it is practical and appropriate during instruction and assessment experiences.

Figure 4.12   Work Preference Survey

1. I prefer to work with _____ because _____

2. I do not like to work with _____ because _____

3. I would rather work _____ alone _____ with a partner _____ with a small group

4. My favorite type of group assignment is _____ because _____.

5. My favorite type of partner assignment is _____ because _____.

6. My favorite type of independent assignment is _____ because _____.

7. The best thing about group work is _____.

8. The worst thing about group work is _____.

9. The place I would rather work in this classroom is _____.

Other Comments _____

4. Learn to Be an Observer

Digging Deep Into Assessment

Break an observation into manageable parts by looking at the different levels of a student's performance related to a standard. Use the vertical scale in Figure 4.13 to mark the student's knowledge and performance level. This differentiated assessment view reflects the student's breadth and depth of understanding.

After the student's performance level is identified in relation to a grade-level standard, use the assessment data to plan the next step of instruction on the student's readiness level.

Figure 4.13   Looking at Performance From Lowest to Highest

Lowest-Performing Level

1. The teacher shows several pictures and says, "Find the picture of the _____." The student points to the picture.

2. The teacher shows a picture, and the student identifies it orally.

3. The teacher shows a picture. The student identifies the picture and gives details about it from his or her background and experiences.

4. The teacher provides the picture. The student matches the picture to the written identification label.

5. The teacher provides the word. The student draws a matching picture.

6. The teacher provides the picture. The student writes the word.

7. The teacher orally presents the word. The student writes, illustrates, and explains the term.

Highest-Performing Level

While Observing and Assessing

Be observant while working with individuals, small groups, or moving around the classroom among the students. Use the observed information to plan instruction and assessment activities. Intervene with appropriate probing questions to identify areas of success and places for improvement. Ask open-ended questions so learners express and explain what they know. Give specific praise and feedback as needed.

Be aware of areas that indicate a need for modification such as the following:

- An intervention or reteaching
- A more challenging assignment
- More time to solve problems and to process
- Faltering or failing to complete the task
- Viewing information from a different angle or innovative way
- Generation of new ideas

Observation Tips

Ask yourself the following:

- Is the student capable of communicating his or her thinking?
- Is the student rushing carelessly through the steps?
- Did the learner correctly verbalize his or her inside thinking to process the steps or procedures?
- Who needs extra help or a specific intervention?
- Who needs to move on to the next challenging step?
- Which specific behaviors need an anecdotal comment?

PERFORMANCE-LEVEL TITLES FOR THE ASSESSED LEARNER

Novice, apprentice, practitioner, and *expert* are terms often used in rubrics and Likert scales to identify the progress of student performance at the time of the measurement. Consider the following explanations and needs as you assist learners on each performance level.

Provide novice learners with the information they need to fill in the gaps of the background knowledge necessary to learn the new information. Students at the other levels are able to solve the problem. They find solutions on their level of understanding, in their own way. As they learn more and gain confidence, their responses become more sophisticated. The strategies and activities are designed to fit the learner's readiness level.

As students develop in their knowledge base, they are able to adapt the information and apply it to real-life situations. This information and experience becomes a part of their memory banks. The teacher analyzes the data to see who needs to move on to a new piece of learning and who needs extended practice. Reflections are used continually to review and revise effective assignments.

Involve students as active participants in making assessment decisions. For instance, ask one of the following questions:

What parts do you know and understand?

What do you need next?

Look for opportunities to give learners ownership in decisions that affect their improvement and growth. This encourages students to practice self-reflection techniques. Let them know how their suggestions influence planning.

Assessing Previous Performance

Consider waiting until a student has been in your classroom a few weeks before delving into achievement records from the previous year. This allows you to develop a picture of a learner's abilities and skills without preconceived ideas. Keep in mind that a student often exhibits different attitudes and levels of effort with each teacher.

Airasian (2011) uses the term *hearsay* in reference to comments from others about a student. Individuals who make statements related to a student's background, ability, or behavior usually have good intentions. They believe the information prepares the new teacher for the student. Listen, and then carefully screen the information embedded in the statements. Some informal comments may provide vital data that impact assessment performance. Think positively when you encounter negative statements containing phrases similar to the following (Figure 4.14):

Figure 4.14 Assessing Behavioral Comments	
When Someone Says . . .	*Use These Self-Reminders . . .*
He is so bad that he	A student usually behaves for me.
His entire class has always been	I develop a positive classroom culture.
His parents won't	Parents become my partners in teaching.
You will never get him to	I'll find ways to motivate him.

Apply What You Know About a Student

Be cognizant of the student's current knowledge, success, and progress. Develop a collection of diagnostic tools to gather data related to individual students. Carefully analyze the data. Mentally prepare for a myriad of possible needs. Unexpected gaps in learning may arise, but if you are ready to assist with the most common needs and are prepared to provide immediate feedback and guidance, the student will benefit. Be thoroughly familiar with various differentiated assessment strategies and tools so you can diagnose problems, gather personal data, and promptly assist the learner.

SUMMARY

Most effective formative assessments are designed to know students as people and learners. These results form the basis for planning. Continuously monitor progress before, during, and after learning to guide instruction. Recognize the individual learner's need, provide interventions, clarify directions, and motivate students. In future chapters, we will examine ways to incorporate this knowledge of students into differentiated assessment strategies.

EXPLORING
SELF-ASSESSMENT

Essential Question: How does self-assessment enhance achievement?

A student has the opportunity for personal reflection to identify and be accountable for understanding strengths, needs, and weaknesses.

WHAT IS SELF-ASSESSMENT?

Self-assessment is a thinking process that provides the learner with a personal guidance system before, during, and after tasks. This metacognitive action enables individuals to analyze as well as think creatively and critically. Each aspect of the self-assessment process provides continuous positive or negative feedback. Self-assessment is a skill that can be used throughout life as learners move toward personal and academic goals.

WHAT IS SELF-TALK?

Self-talk is internal dialogue that elicits a response to external conditions. It creates a continuous flow of thought controlling emotions, feelings, attitudes, decisions, and actions. Self-talk guides metacognitive thinking processes in all aspects of life.

> The most effective learners are metacognitive: That is, they are mindful of how they learn, set personal learning goals, regularly self-assess and adjust their performance, and use productive strategies to assist their learning.
>
> —Tomlinson and McTighe (2006, p. 79)

WHAT IS THE ROLE OF SELF-TALK IN SELF-ASSESSMENT?

When learners use self-talk productively, they can monitor their thinking before, during, and after assignments including assessment tasks. It is a personal monitoring system that guides self-assessment. Self-talk is a natural phenomenon that occurs automatically. With instruction and guidance, students can engage in the activities, while thinking about their thinking, analyzing their self-talk, and using it in productive ways.

To work with a student's self-talk, the learner must reveal his or her thinking. Strategies such as questioning techniques can be used by the individual to probe the mind.

When negative feedback is evident in self-talk, students often shut down and give up. They can learn to recognize unconstructive thoughts and use specific strategies to channel their thinking in positive directions.

PRODUCTIVE METACOGNITIVE CONDITIONS

The learning climate has to be conducive to thinking. Be consciously aware of the aspects of instruction that create productive metacognitive processes. Quality thinking occurs when differentiated activities and assignments are as follows:

| challenging | interesting | relevant | valuable | useful |
| needed | intriguing | novel | memorable | personalized |

Assessing the Learner's Internal Dialogue

A student's internal dialogue is often evident in his or her body language. Analyze the actions. Address the feelings and needs, as soon as possible, in personal conferences and customized instructional plans. Use the following chart (Figure 5.1) as a guide to assess internal dialogue. Of course, actions will occur that do not appear on this list. Add the behavior, the probable self-talk taking place, and your analysis as it is observed.

Figure 5.1 Assessing Internal Dialogue		
Observed Action	*Analysis*	*Learner Self-Talk*
No buy-in	Sees no personal gain or value Lacks interest	*This is not for me.* *I am wasting my time.*
Defeated/ quitter	Gives up No effort exerted Did not complete the assignment	*I cannot do this.* *This is too hard for me.* *If I do this, I will fail.*
Lost	Needs clear directions Lacks background	*What do I need to do?* *I don't know what to ask.*
Unprepared	Does not have needed materials Did not complete the assignment	*I forgot to do this.* *I didn't study.*
Unchallenged	No desire to complete it Hurries through the task Approaches the task in a halfhearted manner.	*This is too easy.* *This is not worth my time.* *I have better things to do.*
Dependent	Accustomed to help Lack of confidence	*Someone will help me.* *It won't be correct if I complete it.*
Underachiever	Not working to potential Lacks initiative	*I tried, but I give up.* *Whatever I do, it will be wrong.*

SELF-TALK FOR TASK ASSESSMENT

Teach students how to be self-directed, independent learners before, during, and after an assignment or task. Teach students how to apply self-talk assessment by selectively choosing the appropriate questions for the individual's needs and the assignment from the following list. Discuss and model the thinking processes that accompany each selected question.

This procedure is easily compared to a pilot's preparation for take-off, system maintenance during the flight, and a safe landing. When students learn how to apply self-assessment strategies automatically, they become more efficient and successful in their academic and personal tasks.

Before Task Engagement

Before engaging in a task or assignment, the student addresses and answers questions similar to the following:

- What is the purpose or outcome of the assignment?
- Do I understand the directions or guidelines?
- What classroom rules will I need to follow?
- What will I learn or gain from this experience?
- Do I have the proper background and/or skill to perform this task?
- What is the amount of time allotted for this assignment?
- Do I have the materials I need?
- Do I have adequate space to concentrate and work comfortably?
- Should I create a plan to carry out the task?
- Do I need to use a graphic organizer, a timeline, an outline, or a "to do" list?
- Do I need to clarify my thoughts or ask questions?
- Do I need more information from the following:

    Teacher   Classmates   Resources

During Task Engagement

- How am I doing?
- Does this continue to be challenging?
- Do I need encouragement to continue?
- Am I putting forth my best effort?
- Am I on the right track?
- Am I following the timeline or pacing my work?
- Have I spent too much time and energy on this section?
- Am I bogged down?

- Am I going in the right direction?
- Do I need help?
- Do I need more information?
- Do I need additional materials or resources?
- Have I completed parts of the assignment that I know I can do, so I have more time to work on the segments that require more thinking?

After the Task

When time is available immediately following an assignment, students need to know to use this time wisely. The following questions will guide their constructive self-talk:

- Did I follow directions?
- Which items or parts . . .
  - are correct and need to be left alone?
  - need more information?
  - are wrong and need to be corrected?
  - need a review?
  - are blank and need my best guess?
- What do I need to ask for clarification or guidance?
- How would I explain this to others so they understand it?
- Which segments need more clarification?
- Which information do I need to retain and recall?
- What memory clues will help me remember important details or steps?
- What did I learn from this assignment?
- Did I reach my goal?

Reflections

Use the questions or open-ended statements at the end of an assignment as journal activities, a bridge for yesterday's work, or as a ticket out the door. When students experience these self-talk opportunities, they learn the value of reflection and begin to use self-talk automatically as an internal tool.

When a task is complete and turned in, the learner benefits from self-talk. The following prompts will continue the learner's internal dialogue:

- What did I learn from this experience that will help me improve in future tasks?
- Next, I need to _____.
- What emotions did this evoke? Why did I have this reaction?
- Which segments of the completed task need _____?

  More help   Review   Practice   To remember

- Which responses are correct?
- How did my feelings and attitude affect my work?
- The tips or suggestions I need to share with my teacher to improve my work in the next assignment are _____.

TEACHING SELF-ASSESSMENT

Self-assessment gives the learners a sense of ownership and responsibility. Pride develops as individuals see how much they have learned from the entry point through the end of the study. Involving them in the assessment process improves learning.

Strategically plan to engage students in daily assessment opportunities. When students are involved in creating and planning activities, their confidence increases. They are motivated to continue learning and to want to do more. Emphasize achievement rather than failure and defeat (Stiggins, 2011). This promotes an *I can do . . . !* attitude instead of *I don't get it!* Each successful step moves students from their current positions toward their learning goals. They need to ask themselves the following questions:

- What do I need next to accomplish this goal or task?
- What help do I need?
- How can I close the gap?

The answers to self-assessment questions become guides to the next steps in learning. Pupils of all ages can learn to self-assess. The process provides opportunities for monitoring and communicating their progress (see Figure 5.2).

Figure 5.2 Learning Performance Levels		
Level	*Performance Indicators*	*Needs*
Novice	Little or no understanding of information Limited background or foundation	Needs background to be ready for new learning
Apprentice	Demonstrates some understanding of information Has some background experience	Ready for the task
Practitioner	Shows understanding of the concepts Easily applies new information and skills	Needs alternative applications and practice of the task
Expert	Demonstrates a deep understanding and can explain what, why, and how Able to apply information to other situations	Needs a more challenging version of the task

Why Is It Important to Teach Learners How to Self-Assess?

In data-driven classrooms, emphasis is often placed on completing work on time, products, and grades. Self-assessment places the student in the driver's seat to monitor and control his or her progress, success, and needs. When students self-assess, they are able to quickly turn mistakes into learning opportunities. They become independent and responsible for their own learning.

SELF-CHECKING TECHNIQUES FOR ASSESSMENT

Provide various opportunities for students to create a personal self-check toolbox. Introduce each self-check technique by talking through the expectations and the process step by step. This approach can be used while checking papers with the total group, alone, with a partner, or small group. Model and practice each one until mastery is evident. Revisit and use it occasionally in daily activities. Individuals are responsible for checking their own work.

Total Class: Using Self-Checking

Teachers spend endless hours checking papers that will not receive a value for the grade book. Use time more productively by using teacher-directed checking sessions. Students not only learn to identify the correct and incorrect answers, they also learn to process the rationale for their answers. Use the following procedure often so students see the value of self-checks and learn the steps.

Select the best papers to use to teach the technique by applying the following tips:

- Select papers that are not going to receive a score for the grade book.
- Use an assignment that needs a review or explanation. Be sure it is a productive use of time to build knowledge.
- Select work completed by students during class time.
- Avoid using homework to teach self-checking procedures because students have often received assistance with the answers.

Procedure for Total Class Self-Checking

Use the following steps to teach students to correct answers when they look over their papers and complete work:

1. Have each student check his or her own papers using a writing implement that writes in a different color. For example, green ink represents "growing."

2. Go over each answer.

3. Call on a student who has the correct answer to explain his or her thinking process.

4. As the answer is revealed and explained, the learner leaves it alone, if it is correct. If it is wrong, the student draws a line through it and writes the correct response above it. In this step, individuals learn how to identify errors and correct mistakes.

5. Do not collect papers, but direct students to place them in a portfolio, notebook, or take-home folder.

Alone: Using Self-Checking

Check It Out Station

Create a Check It Out Station or checking spot as a designated area where students check their work with an answer key. Post the answer key in several areas of the room so one student can stand and check work immediately following completion of the assignment. They receive feedback without waiting for someone to find the time to check it (Chapman & King, 2008).

Stock the station with the answer sheet and only one novel, intriguing writing implement. Do not allow pencils in the checking area. Admit one student in the area to correct work. The learner identifies the incorrect responses, draws a line through the error, and writes the correct response directly above it. Place a note in the checking area with directions telling the student where to place the paper after it is corrected.

Variations:

- The checker chooses three colored pens and completes a marking key similar to the following:

  Green = My corrections!

  Purple = My opinions!

  Yellow = Spotlights my best work on this assignment!

- Match the special checking tools with the topic of study. For example, in a study of plants, supply green gel pens. In a study of historical documents, attach a feather to a pen to represent a quill, or roll paper to create a scroll.

The greatest value of the Check It Out Station is for the student to view areas of strength and weaknesses while actively engaging in self-correcting. Levine (2002) emphasizes the value of immediate feedback. As students take responsibility for checking work, they develop confidence and a sense of independence, learn to self-assess, and become self-regulated learners. Of course, the Check It Out Station reduces the amount of paperwork for adult grading.

Challenge students to create another name for the Check It Out Station such as the following:

Correct Spot	Correction Zone	Is That Your Final Answer?
Mistake Remover Zone	Bus Stop Station	Survivor Checkpoint

Reward students with opportunities to become the next Check It Out assistant, checker, or analyst. When students become productive in using the station, challenge them to design a new checking key and select special checking tools.

Partners: Using Self-Checking

Analyzing and checking work with a partner is a valuable strategy to incorporate in any classroom. During this process, explain the following rule to make this a productive work session. No swapping of papers, please! Students read, work, and correct their own paper or work so they receive immediate feedback.

Partner Checking Directions

1. Students select a partner, or the teacher assigns team members.

2. Each learner brings the completed assignment to a designated workspace and joins a partner to compare, check, and discuss answers.

3. The partner team reads over the paper and identifies items with the same answers.

4. When answers are different, partners discuss the responses and come to consensus on the right answer. The individual who answered correctly explains his or her thinking process.

5. Partners discuss why the response is incorrect and make needed corrections.

6. Add more to an answer, if additions are discovered during the discussion.

7. After completing the activity, partners return to their seats with a better understanding of the correct responses and an understanding as to why errors were made.

Small Group: Using Self-Check

Students join a group of three to four students for a discussion of an open-ended statement or question. This discussion exposes each learner to other details and possible answers for responses. Also the group can talk about parts that they do not believe are accurate; adjust to make them correct after a discussion to come to a consensus.

Most of the time a student answers the question and the teacher reads the entry answer, gives it a grade, and returns it to the student. In turn, the student looks at the grade and moves on to the next task. This involves sharing answers, hearing additional input, and discussing which parts are right and wrong while processing the information. One major benefit of this is that they hear different points of view, other entry statements and details, and have a chance to share their answers with others while analyzing the strengths and weaknesses of their work.

Small-Group Checking Directions

1. Form discussion groups with three or four students.

2. Have each learner bring completed open-ended questions to a designated work area.

3. Supply marking pencils for each student to write corrected notes on their papers.

4. Have each learner read his or her entry followed by a discussion of the accurate and incorrect responses. Students make needed additions to their individual work.

5. Celebrate and thank the partner for sharing.

ASSESS ON-TASK BEHAVIORS

Use the following chart (Figure 5.3) to become acquainted with the students' characteristics as dependent and independent learners. Use the information to develop the behaviors they need for success in academic and personal activities.

> My heart is singing for joy this morning. A miracle has happened! The light of understanding has shone upon my little pupil's mind, and behold, all things are changed!
>
> —Annie Sullivan

Figure 5.3   Dependent and Independent Behaviors
Dependent Behaviors
• Has little or no prior experience • Lacks strategies and skills • Has difficulty comprehending oral or written directions • Exhibits little or no persistence • Does not try when tasks become difficult • Lacks memory skills to retain and recall directions, skills, formulas, and rules • Depends on others for assistance and guidance
Independent Behaviors
• Monitors his or her own learning • Paces work based on difficulty and time allotted • Uses self-reflection to identify needs • Knows and applies various strategies • Requests assistance as a last resort • Applies memory strategies • Works without assistance

SUMMARY

Anxiety and stress may block or interrupt concentration so deeply that students exhibit dependent behaviors while working on assigned tasks. If learners have adequate background knowledge and experience, they are more likely to exhibit independence. Students who become self-regulated and self-directed in their approaches to assessment tasks are more likely to demonstrate initiative and responsibility.

FORMATIVE ASSESSMENT BEFORE THE LEARNING 6

Essential Question: How will preassessment tools optimize planning for individual needs?

Preassessment is an essential component of planning to meet the diverse needs of learners in a differentiated classroom. The goal of preassessment is to expose each learner's prior knowledge, skills, interests, and feelings before the information is presented. The analysis and examination of the gathered data becomes the guide for the planning blueprint. This chapter provides information with a variety of formative assessment tools, formal and informal, to assess before learning. It also presents practical, take-to-the-classroom activities for assessment.

Preassessment is an essential prerequisite for effective diagnosis and planning. Preassess the learner's knowledge base and experiences in relation to the upcoming topic, standard, or skill. Administering an appropriate preassessment is the key. Preassess one to three weeks before beginning the unit of study, so data collected can be used during planning. Use the information gathered to establish the starting point for planning learning experiences to design interventions and identify needed resources. Strategically administer preassessments before planning lessons to address the students' strengths and needs during instruction.

Consider the value of preassessment presented in the following scenario: A physical education teacher is gathering information to develop lesson plans to teach volleyball. A preassessment reveals that a few students have no knowledge or experiences in relation to the sport. Their exposure to the game needs to begin with the fundamentals. Other students know the basics of the game, the rules and regulations, and understand their role. They engage in activities that perfect specific skills. These learners review the techniques, rules, and practice, but they do not need to learn the fundamentals of the game. The information would be boring and disengaging, and more importantly, their valuable time is better spent learning more complex skills. A third group of students, who play the game regularly and are proficient with the skills, need to participate in activities to improve their speed and accuracy. This scenario applies to most learning situations across grade levels in all content areas. See Figure 6.1.

Figure 6.1 Adjusting Assignments

Example: Physical Education		Subject: Knowledge Base of Volleyball
Levels	*Assessment Diagnosis*	*Prescriptions*
Level I Green *Growing*	Possesses little or no knowledge or experiences in relation to the sport	Learn how to play the game. Introduce rules and regulations. Understand the positions and roles.
Level II Yellow *Ray of Sunshine*	Ready for the basics of the game Has been exposed to the rules and regulations of the game Understands the different roles or positions	Review the techniques. Review rules. Practice the skills for each position. Play the game.
Level III Red *All Fired Up!*	Is ready to play the game as a team member Possesses the knowledge and skills to play the game	Improve individual speed and accuracy. Extend and enrich skills. Explore related areas opportunities.

Source: Adapted from Chapman and King (2008).

Strong preassessments reveal the following about the individual student:

- Knowledge base and background experiences related to the standard or skill
- Attitudes, likes, and dislikes
- Feelings and emotions
- Interests and talents
- Strengths and weaknesses
- Entry point for new information

An appropriate preassessment process eliminates wasted time and energy during instruction. This process includes the following steps:

1. Thoroughly examine vital parts of the upcoming lesson or unit.

2. Identify the targeted standards, skills, and concepts.

3. Select the most efficient assessment tool to pinpoint each individual's knowledge before the learning.

4. Administer the preassessment before planning.

5. Gather and interpret the data.

6. Use the data to differentiate instructional plans.

Making each lesson meaningful for all learners is a challenging and rewarding task. Continuously assess students' readiness to identify the next steps in a procedure, to move to the next level, demonstrate mastery of the standard, or to approach new skills or concepts. The term *readiness* means "prepared." The state of readiness, or entry point, for a new skill, standard, or concept opens the door to the learner's success. The following question is answered in an effective preassessment:

> Teach by doing whenever you can and only fall back upon words when doing it is out of the question.
>
> —J.-J. Rousseau (1762)

Does this learner know how to _____ before we begin _____?

PERSONALIZE INSTRUCTIONAL PLANNING

Formative, differentiated assessment allows teachers to personalize or customize instructional plans for individual learners. A variety of preassessment tools are used to gather data about students so crucial information is available to strategically design plans. Continuously strive to create a positive environment that is physically, emotionally, and socially tailored to the needs of individuals.

It is important to identify the student's attitudes or mind-sets toward an upcoming topic or subject. Everyone avoids unpleasant experiences, so negativity is a formidable barrier to success. When learners experience negative thoughts and attitudes, their desire to work on assigned tasks is diminished.

The familiar adage "You can lead a horse to water, but you can't make him drink" can be applied to a student's attitude. If an individual has had unpleasant experiences or memories of a situation, a subject, or an activity, it is difficult to change the feelings, rebuild confidence, and create the desire to engage in a related assessment task. Return to the saying about the horse. You may not be able to make him *drink*, but you can make the horse very *thirsty* if you feed him a large amount of sweet oats! In a similar way, kindle a student's desire to work successfully on assessment activities by providing enticing, meaningful experiences.

How can you discover students' feelings and emotions as they relate to an upcoming topic? The most obvious way is to ask them! The goal is to unleash their individual spontaneous reactions. Select appropriate assessment tools to use before the learning that identify feelings and emotions so specific strategies address these needs. To personalize instructional planning, it is important to know how to use a variety of differentiated assessment tools to collect information about this particular group of students.

Using an assessment preview one to three weeks before designing the lesson plan for the unit builds anticipation, generates interest, and provides personal ownership in learning through the assessment experiences. This targets individual strengths and needs. Think about movie advertisements. Weeks before a movie is released, its previews are accompanied with interviews of the leading actresses and actors.

Promotions appear on billboards, magazines, newspapers, television, radio, and the Internet. It is obvious that this hype is designed to build anticipation and entice patrons. By the time the movie is released, individuals are "hooked." Use this approach to generate excitement and anticipation for new skills, topics, and assessments.

ENGAGING STUDENTS BEFORE THE LEARNING

Student engagement is an important component in all phases of instruction. Engage students in assessment before the learning to . . .

- Identify each individual's background knowledge.
- Present a preview of new learning.
- Target personal strengths and unique needs.
- Discover feelings and attitudes related to the future learning.
- Motivate students and stimulate their desire to learn.
- Identify mastered standards, skills, and concepts.
- Reveal the entry point for the new learning.
- Identify the gaps in background knowledge.
- Create plans for intervention.
- Generate anticipation and excitement for upcoming topics.
- Add novelty and build interest.
- Plan the next steps for each learner.

Formative Preassessment Tools

A formative preassessment tool is a strategically selected, practical technique to provide a view of what a student, small group, or class knows about upcoming information. Select an appropriate tool to show prior learning. Be sure the tools are efficient, easy to view, and provide immediate feedback results before the learning.

The following thirteen preassessment tools and activities reveal the learner's knowledge base and prior experiences related to the topic. Use the gathered data to plan differentiated instruction.

1. Ponder and Pass

Announce the topic of the upcoming unit or skill. Pass a piece of paper with the following graphic organizer (Figure 6.2) to members of the class. Challenge students to write the facts they know related to the topic. They may include information they want to learn and explore, including questions and comments of interest or concern. Encourage students to submit other categories and headings for future

Ponder and Pass activities. The following activity is a way to obtain learner input for an upcoming topic. This paper can be passed around the room to gather this vital information.

Figure 6.2 Ponder and Pass			
Topic _____			
Facts We Know	Information We Want to Learn	Our Questions to Explore	Other Comments

2. Signal and Action Responses

Use this individual response technique to gather informal data in this quick, engaging format. With each of the following examples, a learner chooses one action to fit his or her appropriate knowledge-base level.

Example A

Waving hands ⟶ *I know it.*

Shrug of shoulders ⟶ *I have a hunch.*

Thumbs down ⟶ *I have no idea.*

Example B

Point to your brain ⟶ *I know it.*

Point to your eyes ⟶ *I have seen this before.*

Cover your ears ⟶ *I have never heard of it!*

3. Take a Stand

In the Take a Stand preassessment activity, students move to a number that represents their knowledge base for a topic or skill. The teacher observes the learners' selected positions to gather information. The group at each number discusses and defends their position. Each group shares a summary of their findings with the total class. An analysis of the class discussion serves as a valuable preassessment tool.

Directions

1. Place large numbers from one to six in order around the room.

   Option: Also add a large piece of chart paper near each number to record key discussion notes.

2. Separate the numbers so there is space for a group of students to line up in front of or gather around the displayed numbers.

   Variation: Some grade levels and topics require fewer numbers.

3. Post and state the essential question, standard, fact, topic, or opinion for discussion.

4. Give the following directions to students:
   a. Think about your knowledge of _____.
   b. On a scale of one to six, rate your knowledge of this topic. Example: Six is the expert level; one is the novice level.
   c. At your desk, secretly record the rating of your knowledge on a piece of paper. Add your rationale for selecting this number.

      Note: Students will be less likely to change positions to be with friends when they record their position choice on paper.

   d. Stand in front of the number that represents your knowledge level.
   e. Discuss why you chose the position with the group.
   f. Select a group spokesperson to share the discussion ideas and findings. *Optional:* Create a pictograph with the Take a Stand data by drawing a stick figure to represent each student in each group.

This activity gives students opportunities to demonstrate their understanding and reveals misconceptions related to the topic. Use the discussion details and the rating chart preassessment information to plan future lessons.

4. Knowledge Base Corners

The Knowledge Base Corners (Chapman & King, 2008) activity is an assessment to use before the introduction of a unit to reveal the students' content knowledge. This strategy preassesses upcoming standards or topics. Introduce this activity by exploring hobbies or sports examples. This shows how their knowledge, interests, and experiences vary. When students see this strategy modeled several times and become accustomed to the routine, use it to preassess knowledge of upcoming content. Emphasize that it is acceptable to be in any corner because each position offers a future learning opportunity.

Directions

Display four large strips of paper, and label each one with phrases that match the following four-corner grids. Be creative, and use your content terminology to label the corners. See examples in the figures that follow.

- Post each strip of paper in a corner of the room. Read the corner name aloud.
- Emphasize that this activity will assist to guide plans for their lessons.
- Ask students to write down the name of the corner that matches their knowledge level for the topic.

- Tell students to move to the selected corner to join others with the same view.

- Have each group select a recorder to write on the chart paper. Group members brainstorm information they already know about the topic and what they want to learn.

- Record the brainstormed information and prioritize the items with consensus.

- Call on volunteers from each corner to share findings.

- Tell each group to collectively select a novel way to present the important information on the chart.

- Provide time for each group to report the key discussion points to the class.

Notes: As students stand in their selected corners, observe the number of learners and the information gathered at each knowledge level. Use the data to plan the future unit or topic of study. Assure learners that it is acceptable to be in the novice group because the upcoming information is new.

Variations: When learners know how to use Knowledge Base Corners, add novelty to the activity by changing the phrases on the corner labels to fit the grade level topic information, interests, and backgrounds. See charts in Figures 6.3 through 6.7.

Figure 6.3 Knowledge Base Corners	
Not a clue!	I know a lot!
I know a little bit!	I've got it!

Figure 6.4 Choose Your Team	
Little League	Minor League
Major League	World Series

Figure 6.5 Attitude Corners	
I do not like this.	I like most of it.
I like a few parts.	I like this and cannot wait to learn more.

Figure 6.6 Interest Corners	
Not interested	Occasionally interested
Often interested	Consumed with interest

Figure 6.7 Metamorphosis of a Butterfly	
Egg	Larva
Cocoon	Butterfly

5. Content Knowledge Boxes

Use preassessment activities before a content study unit to uncover what students know and to identify misconceptions they may have. Design content boxes to identify the entry points for planning instruction. Refer to Figure 6.8.

Example

Country _____

We will learn about the areas listed on the chart during our study of (country).

Complete the chart with information you know about (country).

Note: If you do not know specific facts, write what you want to learn.

Figure 6.8 Social Studies

Country _____

Location	Food, Clothing, and Shelter	Resources
Government	Population and People	Customs

Geography	Economy	Historical Landmarks	Ways of Life

United States of America	(Country of Study)

6. Content Surveys

Content Surveys provide information about the background and knowledge base of an individual or group of students. These effective preassessment tools reveal what students know about an upcoming study.

Teacher-created inventories and surveys are best because they are designed for the specific content and students. These assessment tools can be brief and provide needed information. Use surveys as data-gathering tools throughout the year. Ask questions about the specific topic. Include questions and statements that delve into the student's background knowledge, past experiences with the subject, and expectations or goals related to the learning.

Example: Preassessment Survey

- How does _____ relate to you?
- What do you want to learn about _____?
- What do you know about the upcoming study?
- How do you feel about _____? Why?
- What do you hope we do during the study?
- What are you excited about learning? Why?
- Identify the part(s) you are dreading. Why?

7. Personal Surveys and Inventories

Personal inventories and surveys provide information about the life of a student. The gathered information reveals the learner's interests, emotions, feelings, likes, dislikes, dreams, and goals. These factors have a direct impact on a student's approach to learning, engagement, and personal performance level.

Examples

- List your favorite _____.
- What is your least favorite?
- Name a peer who is a favorite working partner.
- Where do you like to study?

8. Brainstorming

Use brainstorming to give students a voice in planning an upcoming topic. Use questions similar to the following to gather data related to what the students already know about a standard, concept, topic, or unit of study. Use the following examples to design your brainstorming probes.

- List the terms, facts, or concepts you know about our new topic.
- What have you heard about this subject in other classes? When and where?
- I have heard about _____ in the following _____ (books, Internet sites, or articles).
- How have you used this information in your world?
- How do you feel about learning _____? Why?

9. Color Clusters

The following Color Cluster activity uses a color key to identify students' levels of knowledge related to a topic. Give each learner a set or cluster of colored disks made from construction paper to match a key similar to the one here. Ask each student to display the color reflecting his or her level of learning for a particular skill or topic.

Example Key

Green = On the launch pad

Yellow = Cautious

Red = Moving on up

Blue = Soaring

10. Gallimaufry Gathering

Assign this activity a week or two before the study begins. Tell students they are going to create a topic or unit gallimaufry, or hodgepodge of various things. Place the topic on the outside of a box, bucket, tub, crate, or shelf. Challenge students to become scavengers, discoverers, and investigators to find the solutions and answers to a posed problem or question related to the upcoming topic, skill, or event. Encourage learners to fill the container with written materials recorded on the Gallimaufry Gathering Grid related to the topic.

Learners find the resources or information in various media, across many genres. Suggest ways to find information including interviews, magazine articles, newspaper clippings, web searches, or television shows. The teacher and students need to screen the selected material for accuracy. Create an entry form for students to complete when they contribute to the collection (see Figure 6.9). This enhances the learning

Figure 6.9   Gallimaufry Gathering Grid

Name _____

Topic _____

1. I found _____

_____

2. It tells _____

_____

3. We can use it to _____

_____

_____

Signature: _____

Date: _____

Resources: _____

atmosphere as students develop a feeling of ownership in the new learning experience. Use the collection as a resource to enhance the unit of study.

Variation: Add novelty to the collection process by changing the title. The following suggestions are motivational, creating the desire to complete the task.

Mystery Masters	Search and Seize	Dig and Delve
Mind Time Probing	Be Sherlock!	Operation Explorer

11. ELOs

Evening Learning Opportunities (ELOs) (Chapman & King, 2009a) are after-school challenges that build knowledge and background while supporting learning. These assignments challenge learners to be detectives, scavengers, investigators, and inventors. An ELO is not homework. It is an opportunity that does not receive a grade. These tasks often require higher-order thinking skills. The goal of using ELOs is for students to gain background knowledge related to an upcoming standard, skill, or concept.

ELO Examples From Content Areas

Math

- Go on a scavenger hunt in your kitchen to find items packaged in pint, quart, gallon, or liter containers. Make a list of the items for each size.

- Be a detective, and locate a recipe that uses a tablespoon, a teaspoon, and a cup to measure ingredients. Bring a copy of the recipe to class to share.

- Find examples of the following shapes in your neighborhood: circles, squares, triangles, and ovals. Make a list of the items with the names of the shapes they represent.

Science

- Create a drawing to show how you classify and categorize the list of animals.

- Create a chart to show the categories of food in your kitchen or items in your garage.

- List animals found in your neighborhood and home. Label them as mammals, fish, birds, reptiles, or amphibians.

Physical Education

- Observe a baseball, football, basketball, or soccer team. Compare and contrast the major strengths and weaknesses, specific skills, or sportsmanship exhibited.

- If you participate in a sport, in sequential order list the activities you engage in to get ready for a game.

Social Studies

- Interview a parent, neighbors, or others about the requirements for their jobs. Identify their skills and work habits.

- Review a movie or documentary based on the country you are studying. Create a chart to show the advantages and disadvantages of living in that country.

Language Arts

- Watch a sitcom or newscast. Record the main ideas and supporting details.

- Watch a game show, or play a game. Write the sequence of events.

12. Pretest

A pretest is a formal assessment given before planning to gather vital information to customize instruction. The test reveals the background and knowledge base of each class participant. A well-developed pretest saves time because the data reveal the learner's needs before planning designed instruction. Instruction is not hit or miss but on target.

Developing the Pretest

Design the pretest to provide a comprehensive overview that addresses the simple to complex essentials. It takes time to strategically develop a pretest. However, it is a valuable tool when the findings guide formative differentiated instruction.

Use the following guidelines to create an effective pretest (Chapman & King, 2008):

- Administer the preassessment one to three weeks before teaching the new topic or unit. This provides time for the data gathering, analysis processing, and using the results in curriculum planning.

- Design the test items so no one can achieve a 100 or 0 percent score. Select items to challenge each learner taking the test.

- Plan the test to address the various levels of the learners.

- Present items ranging from concrete to abstract and simple to complex.

- Disperse easy and difficult questions or tasks throughout the assessment. This deters students from assuming that the easiest items are at the beginning. Often students stop trying when they come to several consecutive, difficult questions because they assume that the remaining tasks will be more difficult.

- Include manipulatives in the preassessment if they are used in related lessons.

- Use the same pretest as a posttest to analyze growth.

Vary the pretest response formats. For example, use open-ended questions, prompts, graphic organizers, matching, multiple choice, and fill in the blanks. Design the items to challenge learners with easy to complex levels of questions and thinking.

13. Standardized Testing Data

Analyze and interpret previous standardized testing data related to the content material or skills to be addressed. The data are used for making placement decisions and dealing with funding issues, more than academic improvement. Testing information is often overlooked as a valuable resource for planning.

SUMMARY

As learners engage in formative preassessment tasks, their knowledge base expands. They build a foundation for learning with each discovery. Students become responsible for their own learning as they actively participate in preparations for the new topic of study. The hype accompanying preassessment formative activities creates curiosity. Anticipation builds until the topic has its premiere. Create opportunities for students to share the results of their discoveries as a prelude to planning optimal learning opportunities.

FORMATIVE ASSESSMENT DURING THE LEARNING

7

Essential Question: How can various differentiated assessment tools be used for immediate intervention during learning experiences to keep students on track in their learning adventures?

Ongoing formative assessment during the learning experience keeps the learner on track and drives instructional planning. Students learn at different paces using their knowledge, unique skills, ability, and talents. It is essential to select the most effective tool to assess the learner. Assessments during learning provide opportunities to infuse monitoring and adjusting for intervention as a need emerges. It is a major component of the cycle of assessment that is implemented in every segment of learning.

FORMATIVE ASSESSMENT TOOLS TO USE DURING THE LEARNING

The following section identifies some of the most effective tools to use during the learning. Ongoing assessment provides essential information to guide instruction. These vital data guide and customize planning to meet differentiated needs of individual students during the learning process.

Know how to use formative assessment information purposefully and with intent to identify a need for the following:

- planning a variety of instructional strategies
- reteaching, revamping, or enriching
- using flexible grouping
- adjusting an assignment
- providing an alternative resource
- probing or questioning
- providing interventions and extra assistance
- giving specific praise and encouragement

1. Observation

Teacher observation is one of the most effective formative assessment tools. The value of observation is often overlooked in today's data-driven world. Continually search for each learner's level of understanding and personal success with the standard or content information.

Explain the purpose and value of observations to relieve students' anxiety during the data-gathering process. Inform students that notes taken by a teacher or another adult are used to help them learn and improve.

During an observation, data are collected as the learner engages in an activity or assignment. Develop keen visual, auditory, and other perceptual skills to identify a student's academic competency, strengths, needs, abilities, behaviors, social interactions, health, emotions, reactions, feelings, and attitudes. This flexible assessment tool can be used anytime, in any environment, and under any circumstance. Observation data can be used to accomplish the following:

- Document ongoing progress for students, teachers, and parents.
- Record the learner's strengths and weaknesses.
- Identify tasks needed for individuals and groups.
- Assist in planning adjustable assignments.
- Guide selection and monitoring of appropriate resources and materials.
- Support and guide instruction.
- Identify behavior patterns.

2. Anecdotal Assessment

Anecdotal assessment consists of notes that record data to assist or teach the learner. The anecdotal record is the documentation written during observations of a student's work or behaviors.

Recording Anecdotal Notes: A Suggested Procedure

1. Write the student's name, time, activity or subject, and date on top of the note.

2. Record each observation in clear, concise terms.

3. Create a management system that works for you to record observations, such as index cards, self-stick notes, or logs. Each entry needs to record a specific observable behavior.

Tips for Anecdotal Note Observations

With specific data, be sure to record the date and time of the observation. Keep in mind that anything written about a student becomes a public record. Avoid subjective comments and adjectives. Record assessment information, as suggested in the following list in Figure 7.1.

Figure 7.1   Observation Areas

Adapt the following chart to note specific areas while observing the student.

Academic Performance	Behavior
Understandings and misconceptions	Attitude
Following directions	Independence
Strengths and weaknesses	Needs assistance
Successes and failures	Social interactions
Strategies used	Positive and negative behavior
Time on or off task	Attention span
Productivity	Following rules and directions
Knowledge level	Cooperating and/or volunteering
Interests	**Thinking Skills**
Likes and dislikes	Critical thinker
A specific affinity	Creative
Engagement in personal choice	Information retention and processing
Level of motivation	Problem-solving ability

- It is also important to assess the student's ability to cope with particular situations. Record the time, place, and cause of frustration, distraction, or boredom. Remember to assess each learner's ability to work alone, with a partner, or in a small group.

- During an observation, be alert to the learner's needs. Successes must be noted and praised. The most valuable notes contain assessment data to analyze what, how, why, and when this student is learning. Use the information to intervene and design instruction for the individual.

Variation A: Clipboard Stickies

Use Clipboard Stickies to organize anecdotal notes while assessing a task, action, demonstration, or event by recording specific observable comments. Date the entry, and add the time of day. Document positive and negative behaviors as well as evidence of individual strengths and weaknesses. Identify patterns of behaviors and actions. Include developing and learned habits.

Guidelines for using this assessment strategy:

1. Attach sticky notes to a clipboard.

2. If particular students are to be observed, place each student's name and date at the top of the sticky note. This reminds the observer to strategically observe the notable behaviors and actions of the identified students.

3. Add some blank sticky notes to record observations of unexpected, noteworthy behaviors or skills of other learners.

4. Write notes about the specific behaviors observed. Use consistent note taking to identify behavior patterns.

Variation B: Card Cruising

Use one large index card for each student. Punch a hole in the upper left corner of each card, and place a ring clasp or similar gadget through the hole in the cards to create a quick-flip assessment tool. Write a student's name in the top right-hand corner of the card—for example, *Smith, John*. Alphabetize the cards by first names. Add the student's phone number and other important information in the corner space for easy access. Keep the cards handy to jot down notes from observations.

3. Know it! Show it!

Know it! Show it! provides data on the learner's levels of understanding. The following prompts create varied and inviting ways to spontaneously assess student learning mid-lesson. Know it! Show it! provides students with opportunities to process learning in different ways.

- Tell a partner, and compile the answers.
- Say the correct answer together.
- Come to consensus as a group and create your platform.
- Tab the answer with a sticky note flag.
- Place a game piece on the answer.
- Demonstrate with a manipulative.
- Role-play to create a simulation.
- Demonstrate and tell the process you used.
- Tell your step-by-step procedure.
- Mark it in your class notes using a unique symbol or font.
- Point to the answer or example on/in a

graph	book	transparency	bulletin board
passage	picture	diagram	document reader
text	sentence	journal	chart
SMART Board	computer		

Use a choice board like the following (in Figure 7.2) during a Know it! Show it! assessment. This provides learners with the opportunity to choose their favorite way to show what they know. The Know it! Show it! assessment directions may be adapted for a cube activity.

Figure 7.2 Know it! Show it! Choice Board Sample		
Create an example.	Illustrate it.	Place it on a graphic organizer.
Put it to a beat.	Show it.	Write it.

4. Response Cards

Response cards are effective and engaging formative assessment tools. They can be used to quickly and efficiently assess before, during, and after instruction. They assist the teacher in gauging the learners' prior knowledge, interest, confidence, or anxiety on a topic. Response cards also give students valuable practice in metacognition, or thinking about their own thinking.

The cards are made with two or more possible answers. Students choose a response by pointing to their answer. As seen in the following examples, response cards are highly adaptable instruments. The following samples are designed as informal preassessment activities. The cards are created with the same response choices written precisely in the same place on the front and back of the card. Tell students to respond by placing their thumb on the response that faces them and the pointer finger on the response facing the teacher. This makes the chosen response visible on each side of the card, so the student and teacher see the selected answer at the same time.

The responses provide the teacher and the student with information about his or her knowledge base, background, feelings, emotions, attitudes, likes or dislikes, facts learned, and misconceptions (see Figure 7.3). During learning experiences, use response cards to reveal feelings and understanding. During a review or cumulating activity, revisit the cards as post-assessment tools that reveal changes in the student's feelings, attitudes, interests, and academic knowledge.

After a card is made and used the first time, have the students turn in the cards and add the set to your collection. Place each set in plastic bags, label, and store them for future use. Keep extra blank cards handy to replace missing or damaged cards.

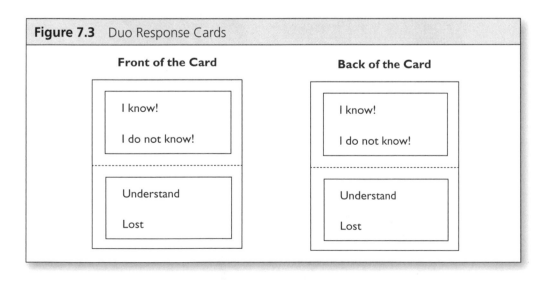

Figure 7.3 Duo Response Cards

Front of the Card

I know!

I do not know!

Understand

Lost

Back of the Card

I know!

I do not know!

Understand

Lost

Have students hold up the response card, and point to or pinch the correct answer. Assess their quickness and accuracy. Observe students carefully as they prepare to respond. If they appear insecure, hesitant, or if they look to classmates for answers, make a mental or written note. Do not tell them to stop looking around or to stop looking at someone else's answer. This behavior is a signal that reteaching or review is needed.

Duo Response Card Possibilities

The level of understanding . . .

I know!	I do not know!
I understand!	I do not understand!
Agree	Disagree
Got it!	Not a clue!
I've got it!	I am lost!
I like this!	I do not like this!
My mind is working!	My mind shut down!
I feel great about this!	This is not working for me.

For content . . .

True	False
Vertebrate	Invertebrate
Fact	Opinion
Cause	Effect

Variation A: Triple Response Cards

Students enjoy the uniqueness of triple responses. The cards are designed so the answer choices appear on the front and back (see Figure 7.4). Use a variety of samples of the cards across topics to engage each student in the assessment.

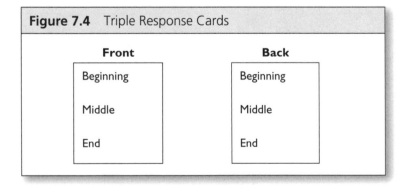

Figure 7.4 Triple Response Cards

Front	Back
Beginning	Beginning
Middle	Middle
End	End

Variation B: High to Low Responses

Use Triple Response Cards to vary the way responses are listed. The following examples use numbers, words, and phrases that range from high to low. This activity quickly reveals where students are in their understanding.

3	2	1
Happy face	Straight face	Sad face
Yes	No	Maybe
I know this	I know some	I am lost
Happy	So-so	Sad
Pluses	Minuses	Still questioning
Agree	Still thinking	Do not agree

Variation C: Low to High Responses

The following number, word, and phrase responses range from low to high:

1	2	3
None	One or two	Three to five
Crawling	Trotting	Racing
Need more time	Checking it over	Finished
Beginning	Middle	End
Do not know	Know a little	Got it
Basement	Middle floor	Penthouse
Bottom of the hill	Climbing up	At the summit

Variation D: Four-Way Response Cards

Modify the directions for the Triple Response Cards by adding one or more words to the card. Remember to write the same words in the same place on the front and back of the card.

Create a variety of new cards for assessment from different topics. Be sure the cards fit the purpose so they show what students know or feel about learning situations and materials (see Figure 7.5).

Figure 7.5   Example of Four-Way Response Cards

Front/Back	Front/Back	Front/Back
A	Never	4. I can explain this!
B	Rarely	3. I am beginning to understand.
C	Sometimes	2. I need to ask a question.
D	Often	1. I do not understand.

Variation E: Content Response Cards

Design response cards as novel, informative tools for assessing specific content. The cards can be used with groups of any size across all content areas. Develop response cards to use in any subject. The following examples are for response cards in selected subject areas (see Figure 7.6).

Figure 7.6   Content Response Cards

Science
- Precipitation
- Evaporation
- Condensation

- Digestive system
- Skeletal system
- Circulatory system

- Mammal
- Reptile
- Amphibian
- Fish

Social Studies
- North
- South
- East
- West

- Mountain
- Desert
- Prairie
- Plateau

History
- World War I
- World War II
- Both

- Mt. Rushmore
- Liberty Bell
- Statue of Liberty

Language Arts
- Descriptive
- Persuasive
- Expository

- Period
- Question mark
- Exclamation point

- Setting
- Character
- Plot

- Adjective
- Adverb
- Verb

Math
- Add
- Subtract
- Multiply
- Divide

- Cube
- Cone
- Sphere
- Pyramid

- Penny
- Nickel
- Dime
- Quarter

---

5. High Five

The High Five assessment tool uses the numbers from one to five to rank personal knowledge level or understanding of the current topic or skill. Name the subject, skill, concept, or topic assessed. Say "1, 2, 3, show me!" Each student shows the appropriate number of fingers as indicators of their level of knowledge and understanding.

5   I understand it and can explain it.

4   I can use it but cannot explain it.

3   I am growing but need help.

2   I am beginning to understand.

1   I am lost.

6. A Bump in the Road

A student writes a problem or question at the top of a piece of paper. The learner passes it to three to five classmates to obtain their suggestions for improvement or answers to the question. Each person initials his or her response to overcome the bump in the road.

7. Color-Coding

Use color-coding to assess steps in a procedure, to organize an agenda, or to highlight items in a list. Involve students in selecting the order of the colors in the sequence. School colors may be used as the first two colors. This helps students remember the beginning sequence. Post the color pattern. Maintain the same color scheme throughout the year in classrooms or schoolwide.

Example

1 = black   2 = blue   3 = green   4 = red   5 = purple

- Color-code with markers, crayons, colored pencils, or construction paper.
- Use the color-coding assessment for the following:
  o Identify steps in a process or procedure.
  o Prioritize a list.
  o Sequence a story, event, or process.

8. Sketches From the Mind

Have students make simple, miniature drawings or sketches of important nouns from the unit or topic of study to use as markers to identify facts or concepts. The drawings provide a mental picture or symbol to locate, remember information, and assess the accuracy of placement.

Examples

In a unit on food study, draw an apple beside each important fact related to fruit.

In a transportation unit with the categories *land, sea,* and *air*, draw a road beside land vehicles, draw waves beside sea vehicles, and draw a cloud beside air vehicles. If the vehicle fits more than one category, use each symbol that matches.

Variation: Label it!

In a math unit that teaches process and procedures, place the operational symbol, such as +, −, ×, or ÷, beside the steps.

In a study of land formations, make stamp-size drawing of confusing terms, such as isthmus and peninsula.

9. Analyzing Student Notes

Students provide valuable information for assessment during learning. When a teacher reads the recorded material, the written words reflect the student's thinking and provide an in-depth view of the learner's interpretation of the information.

Use the following ideas to probe the learner's thinking. The goal is to make the stored information visible for assessment.

Examples

- Highlight important terms or key ideas.
- Tab important or confusing sections of text.
- Write each question or concern on an individual sticky note. Use the note as a flag to identify the source in the notes.
- Draw a box or circle to enclose each key item.
- Place an asterisk or star next to important items.
- Place a check mark to identify key names, dates, events, or specific terms.
- Draw an exclamation point next to the most important facts.
- Place a question mark before a confusing word, phrase, or sentence.
- Write the following responses in notes to highlight important items:

  WOW   Got it   No clue   Duh!   Help   Lost   Yes!   Yee haw!

10. Checkpoint Tests

Use periodic checkpoint tests after reading an important section of the text, after demonstrating a skill, following an introduction of a new procedure, process, or sequence, or presenting a learning segment or important facts needing a quick assessment. Add novelty by selecting the paper size to fit the expected response. For example, use a fourth of a piece of paper for a short answer quiz. The results will show what each student has learned and can apply.

11. Daily Grades

Gather grades from selected daily class assignments, projects, problem-solving opportunities, homework challenges, and pop quizzes. Accumulate grades that reveal a true picture of the individual student's performance. This provides a road map for planning or an immediate intervention.

SUMMARY

It is essential to gather ongoing formative data related to individual student progress. Continuously use formative assessments to avoid pitfalls and struggles that discourage the learner and lead to failure. Use the feedback to reteach, readjust, revamp, enhance, or enrich and customize plans as needed. Teach students how to use self-assessments during learning to develop metacognitive habits and to monitor their own learning. Use a variety of novel assessment tools to excite and stimulate minds during learning.

FORMATIVE ASSESSMENT AFTER THE LEARNING 8

Essential Question: How can various formative differentiated assessment strategies be used after learning to identify the learner's immediate and future instructional needs?

Assessing after the learning traditionally has been viewed as a way to analyze the student's mastery of the standards. Post-assessments are crucial because the results are analyzed to see if the learner has reached the initial goals. If the goals have not been reached, specific plans are customized for this individual. A teacher uses many formative assessment tools to determine whether some or all students need additional experiences in one or more aspects of a study.

STUDENT ENGAGEMENT AFTER THE LEARNING

The formative assessment data after learning are gathered and analyzed to determine the plans for future learning. Engage students in using assessment tools after learning to accomplish the following:

- Reveal mastered information.
- Identify learning gaps.
- Discover needed interventions.
- Pinpoint specific needs for planning the next segment.

Ask yourself the following questions to maintain student engagement:

- When and where am I going to address the identified needs and strengths in the curriculum plan?
- What assessment tools should be used to accommodate this individual?
- How do I keep this learner motivated and wanting to learn?
- What opportunities do I need to provide to challenge this student?
- How can I continue to keep this learner engaged and successful?

ASSESSMENT TOOLS: AFTER THE LEARNING

This chapter explores thirteen effective assessment tools to use after the learning. These evaluative pieces provide data for immediate feedback of progress. This information also is used to plan strategically for future learning opportunities.

1. Effective Questioning Techniques for Formative Assessment

Open-Ended Questions

Open-ended questions challenge students to think and choose their thoughts for the responses. For example, the teacher provides a situation, and the student communicates thoughts and ideas in an answer. It may be in the form of an essential question, hypothesis, or statement. The answers may include many details, an explanation, or a process. This is an important part of formative assessment. If a student uses correct information in a response, he or she shows what is known about the topic. The answer reflects the learner's views and opinions and shows the student's ability to explain the facts or supporting details.

Use the following examples of open-ended questions and probing statements:

Explain how . . .	What is your opinion of . . . ?
What is the reason . . . ?	Describe . . .
Tell more about . . .	Give your step-by-step thinking on . . .
How did you solve this problem?	What happened next?
How can you use the information?	Why is this important?

Reflection Questions

Teach students to use questions for analysis and reflection. Use questioning techniques with journals, reflection activities, on tests, while working with content of a specific topic or unit, or after the learning throughout the day, week, or assignment. Incorporate questions similar to the following in daily lessons and discussions.

Examples

- How many adjustments or changes did you make? Tell me about one of them.
- What obstacles did you overcome?
- What discoveries have you made?
- How will you do this differently the next time?
- What is the most important thing you learned?
- What do you need to learn next?
- Do you have any other comments, suggestions, or concerns?

BLOOM'S TAXONOMY FOR COMPREHENSION ASSESSMENT

Use effective questioning as probes to reveal information the student knows and to identify information he or she needs to learn. The definitions in the next section and Figure 8.1 provide key words for use in developing probing statements, prompts, and questions at various levels of thinking as identified by Bloom and Krathwohl (1956).

Defining the Lingo

Students may be unable to answer open-ended questions because they do not understand the terms in the directions. Provide time for them to discuss and use the most common terms in assessment activities. Explain these key words and definitions in terms students can understand. For example, provide student-friendly definitions of key words found in open-ended questions. Use words from Bloom's Taxonomy.

The following confusing assessment terms are often found in directions and open-ended items. Students can say the word and definition repeatedly to create a rap. Use the catchy definitions to place the terms in long-term memory.

Appraise:	Be the judge!	assess	judge	evaluate
Categorize:	Group it!	classify	sort	group
Elaborate:	Give more details!	say more	expand	give details
Evaluate:	Tell its worth!	conclude	summarize	give its value
Justify:	Take a stand!	explain	defend	give reasons
Illustrate:	Draw it!	show	sketch it	use a picture
Predict:	What will happen?	guess	forecast	expect
Critique:	State your opinion!	account	view	analyze
Formulate:	Put it together!	devise	prepare	set up
Investigate:	Examine it!	explore	inspect	study
Synthesize:	Pull it together!	combine	fuse	blend
Estimate:	Guess! Guess! Guess!	approximate		Give a ballpark figure

Post an ongoing list of the terms in the students' lingo as the words and phrases appear in assessment examples across the curriculum. Use the students' words to create the best definitions. Place the word and its definitions in a rap, song, poem, jingle, chant, or cheer. These exciting experiences motivate learners to retain difficult assessment terms.

Figure 8.1 Key Words From Bloom's Taxonomy		
Levels	*Key Words*		*Classroom Applications*
Evaluation	Judge Value Rate Critique Assess Appraise Summarize Estimate	• Appraise (criticize, conclude) _____ . • Describe the value of this _____. • Evaluate the impact of _____ on _____.
Synthesis	Compose Assemble Construct Design Prepare Arrange Propose Organize Formulate Plan	• Compose (rearrange, compile) _____ . • Use the separate components to create a new _____. • Organize the details to develop a _____.
Analysis	Examine Distinguish Question Identify Differentiate Diagram Criticize Experiment	• Outline (categorize, separate) _____ . • What are the steps in the procedure? • What might happen next? • How do you prove the hypothesis?
Application	Demonstrate Practice Interview Apply Translate Dramatize Operate Schedule Illustrate Interpret	• Demonstrate (operate, show) _____ . • How can you use _____ ? • What ideas and facts support this _____ ?
Comprehension	Describe Restate Explain Identify Report Compare Discuss Recognize Express Review	• Explain (estimate, summarize) _____ . • Describe _____ . • How do you view this _____ ? • What is the author saying?
Knowledge	Define List Repeat Memorize Name Label Record Recall Relate Tell Report Narrate	• Define (recall, recite) _____ . • What is _____ ? • What is the purpose?

Source: Adapted from Bloom & Krathwohl (1956).

2. Post-Sharing Celebrations

A. Wraparound

1. Each class member writes the most important information from the study on a small piece of paper or sticky note.

2. Students bring their notes and join a community group or small circles.

3. The learners take turns sharing one AHA with the rest of the class.

Note: The teacher listens for correct information learned and highlights from the learning.

B. Carousel Gala

1. Hang sheets of chart paper around the room for students to post highlights for a review of a recent unit of study.

2. Write an important heading from the study on each chart paper.

3. Place a dark writing marker at each chart.

4. Divide the class into small groups, matching the number of highlights. For example. If there are 8 charts, divide the class into 8 groups.

5. Assign each small group to a chart. Team members share and write what they know about that topic.

6. Give a signal for the groups to move to the next chart.

7. Tell the new group to read the ideas from the last group and adds more information.

8. Continue to move the groups to each chart around the carousel, as time permits. Remember, it is not necessary for each group to visit every chart.

9. Assign each group one chart. They read, share, and select the favorite information on the poster.

10. Challenge students to present this information in a novel, exciting way for a Carousel Sharing Gala.

C. Rhythmic Fanfare

1. Each small group selects or is assigned a chunk of important information for review.

2. Have each group create a song, poem, jingle, rap, chant or cheer to review and celebrate the selected content information.

3. Provide time for groups to practice and present to the total class.

4. Ask the rest of the class to share what they learned from the musical beat.

5. Celebrate!

3. Likert Scales to Assess Learning, Attitude, and Progress

A Likert scale is a line with graduated numbers, ascending or descending. It is an interval-based multiple-choice assessment instrument. An individual's level of performance is identified using the descriptors for each number on the scale. This scale was originally designed by Rensis Likert, an organizational psychologist.

Create novel scales using words or phrases as indicators and share these with students. Vary the number sequences and terms on the lines, so the learners will be exposed to various directions each time they use the assessment tools (see Figures 8.2 and 8.3).

4. Rubrics: Road Maps to Expectations

Introduce learners to the word *rubric*. It is derived from the Latin word *rubrica*, which means "red." Show students a ruby stone, if one is available. Explain that the earliest uses of the word *rubric* referred to a title, heading, or important passage that appeared in red letters to distinguish it from the less important information.

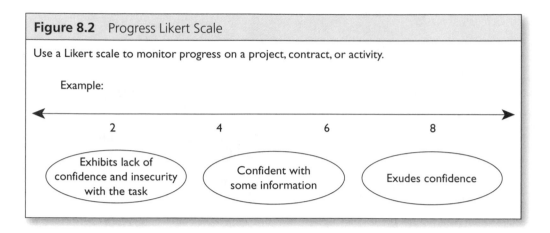

Figure 8.2   Progress Likert Scale

Use a Likert scale to monitor progress on a project, contract, or activity.

Example:

2   4   6   8

Exhibits lack of confidence and insecurity with the task

Confident with some information

Exudes confidence

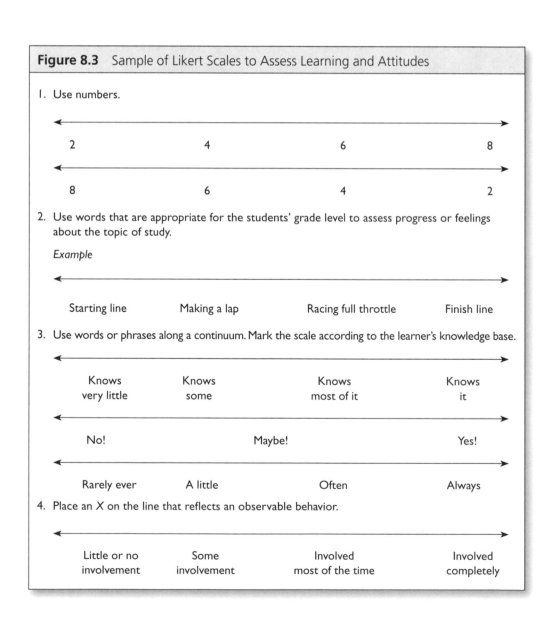

Figure 8.3   Sample of Likert Scales to Assess Learning and Attitudes

1. Use numbers.

    2   4   6   8

    8   6   4   2

2. Use words that are appropriate for the students' grade level to assess progress or feelings about the topic of study.

    Example

    Starting line   Making a lap   Racing full throttle   Finish line

3. Use words or phrases along a continuum. Mark the scale according to the learner's knowledge base.

    Knows   Knows   Knows   Knows
    very little   some   most of it   it

    No!   Maybe!   Yes!

    Rarely ever   A little   Often   Always

4. Place an X on the line that reflects an observable behavior.

    Little or no   Some   Involved   Involved
    involvement   involvement   most of the time   completely

Rubrics commonly used in classrooms today provide the teacher, the student, and parents with the important details for assessment. Each rubric contains an outlined scale. The expectations for a specific task are indicated by the numbers on the scale. The indicators or explanations beside each number on the scale are written in clear terms so the student and teacher can use and understand them.

The best rubric is created by the teacher because it measures what is being taught. When it is feasible, allow students to assist in designing the rubrics. See rubric examples in Figures 8.4–8.9.

Customize the rubrics to assess the following:

specific content	writing sample	skills	behaviors
tasks	responsibilities	oral presentations	standards
projects	demonstrations	teamwork	reports

Figure 8.4   Rubric Template

Student _____ Project _____

Assessor _____ Self _____ Teacher _____ Peer

Project or Product Title	1	2	3	4	Score
Criteria	Descriptors	Descriptors	Descriptors	Descriptors	
Criteria	Descriptors	Descriptors	Descriptors	Descriptors	

Total Score _____

Comments

Understands	Working On	Needs Help

Figure 8.5   Rubric Form

Identify the task of the learners. Write observed student's name and a targeted behavior above each column. Make comments about the observed improvements and the behaviors that are still in progress in the appropriate boxes.

Task _____

Behavior Indicators: What am I assessing and observing?

Student Names	Behavior A	Behavior B	Behavior C
1.			
2.			
3.			
Observed Improvements		**In Progress**	

Figure 8.6   Rubric for a Group Science Project

Topic: Digestive System

Task: Design a display that explains major four major functions of the digestive system.

Name _____

Criteria	4	3	2	1
Layout	Components are proportionate for the design.	The display is appealing. Each part is easy to view.	The display is disorganized. Some parts are difficult to see.	The display is disorganized and unattractive.
Accuracy of Content	Information is accurate.	Most of the information is correct.	A few details are provided, and some information is accurate.	Information is incorrect.
Completeness of Content	All four functions are identified and fully described in an organized format. Detailed descriptions of each function and the interrelationships among them are included.	All four functions are identified and contain some organization. The descriptions use incomplete details.	Two or three functions are described using a few details. The content is disorganized.	All functions are not identified. Descriptions of the functions are incomplete and totally disorganized.
Diagrams/ Graphics	The graphic designs are creative, organized, and clearly explain the topic.	Each graphic explains the topic and is easy to understand.	A few graphics are appropriate and explain the topic.	The graphics are unclear. They do not add understanding to the display.
Appropriate Use of Resources	Five or more resources support the information presented.	Three or four resources support the information.	One or two appropriate resources were used.	No resources were used to support the information.
Teamwork	The student was a valuable team member who worked extremely well with others on all parts of the project.	The student got along well with the team and shared in most of the responsibilities.	The student occasionally interfered with the team's work and permitted others to complete most of the task.	The student did not work as a responsible team member on the project.
Using the Guidelines	All directions and guidelines were followed and completed on this task.	Most steps were completed successfully as directed.	Very few of the project guidelines were followed.	The project guidelines were not followed.

Figure 8.7   Rubric Form Sample for Analyzing an Adjustable Assignment

Name _____ Class/Subject _____ Date _____
Assignment _____

8	Expert _____ _____
6	Knows most of it! _____ _____
4	Knows some information _____ _____
2	Novice _____ _____

Figure 8.8   Rubric Heading Indicators to Describe Success Levels

Does not understand	Can complete task with assistance	Can do some alone	Works independently

1–2 correct	3–5 correct	6–8 correct	9–10 correct

Encounter	Engage	Enhance	Embrace

Figure 8.8 (Continued)

Novice	Apprentice	Journeyman	Master

Can do very little	Can do some	Knows how to do most of the task	Knows how to complete the task

Afraid of this task	Some comfort	Comfortable most of the time	Fearlessly approached this task and comfortably completed it

Dirt road	Paved road	Highway	Yellow brick road

Not a clue	Beginning to understand it	Understands most of it	Got it!

Inadequate response		Satisfactory response		Demonstrates competence

1	2	3	4	5
No attempt to answer	Begins but is unable to complete answer	Minor flaws but satisfactory	Competent response	Exemplary response

Figure 8.9 Progress Rubric

	Organization	Accuracy	Progress
Third Day			
Fifth Day			
Seventh Day			

Weighted Rubrics

A weighted rubric contains a graduated scoring scale. Each number on the scale contains a brief description of the tasks expected and the level of performance. The highest number on the scale usually has a description of high-quality expectations. The lowest number usually contains a description of the lowest task quality and performance accepted in the assignment. This gives each number a weight or value. When learners know the weight or value of each number on the scale, they know the expected criteria. They understand the level of performance required for each scaled number before their work begins. Weighted rubrics take subjectivity out of the grading process and make assessment fair to everyone. All learners have the opportunity to make a high score. See Figure 8.10.

Figure 8.10   Weighted Rubric for a Writing Sample

Student _____ Date _____ Title _____

Evaluator: _____ Self _____ Teacher _____ Peer _____ Parent _____

Scoring Scale: Score each section from 1 to 5.   (low 1   2   3   4   5 high)

Ideas, Content and Organization   **40 points possible**

The ideas and details relate to the same topic.
A central idea is supported with details.
The plot and important points are easy to understand.
The writing has a beginning, middle, and end.
The facts and ideas are purposefully organized.

　　　　Score (low 1   2   3   4   5 high)   Subtotal _____ x 8 = _____

Style and Voice   **30 points possible**

Descriptive words are used appropriately.
Conversation with dialogue is included.
An appropriate voice is used for the reader.
Various types of sentences are included.
Figurative language is used.

　　　　Score (low 1   2   3   4   5 high)   Subtotal _____ × 6 = _____

Word Usage and Sentence Structure   **20 points possible**

The sentences flow and are appropriate.
The verb tense is consistent and correct..
Proper sentence structure is used.
Precise word choice is used.

　　　　Score (low 1   2   3   4   5 high)   Subtotal _____ x 5 = _____

Conventions and Mechanics   **10 points possible**

Mechanical writing enhances reading.
Words are spelled correctly.
Punctuation marks are in place.
Capital letters are used correctly.
The writing is legible.

　　　　Score (low 1   2   3   4   5 high)   Subtotal _____ x 2 = _____

　　　　　　　　　　　　　　　　　　　　　Total = ___
　　　　　　　　　　　　　　　　　　　　　(highest possible score is 100)

Comments:

5. Checklists

Checklists itemize standards, skills, or behaviors to observe or monitor for a specific purpose. The best checklists are created by the teacher, because he or she knows the areas that need to be assessed. These tools are easily customized to meet the needs of the teacher and the student.

The time and energy expended in developing checklists is worthwhile when the tools gather valuable data, provide feedback, and focus instruction on the individual learner's needs.

Use checklists with the following:

- New learning as a process to identify steps completed, understood, or performed
- Behavior management to observe and collect data as a student participates in individual or group experiences
- Centers, projects, experiments, and demonstrations to assess academic needs, on-task behavior, and social interactions

Developing a Checklist

Checklists are practical, flexible assessment tools because they can be designed for a specific subject, activity, skill, or behavior. These instruments can be used during routine activities, and special events. The most valuable checklists assess a learner's skills, knowledge, and attitudes to differentiate instructional plans.

Adapt the following suggested steps to develop a checklist:

1. Choose the purpose of the checklist.

2. Identify the learner(s) to monitor.

3. Brainstorm and list all possibilities to produce a quantity of items.

4. Write each item for the checklist on a separate sticky note.

5. Analyze the list, and reduce it from quantity to quality items.

6. Select the best form to use.

7. Place the quality items in order on the form.

8. Decide who will observe and record the scores. Usually the observer is the teacher, a peer, self, or an assistant. Include a signature line for each observer.

Checklist for the Checklist

Use the following checklist to analyze the format and contents of the checklist assessment tool.

- ❏ Contains observable, clear, specific items
- ❏ Uses an easy-to-score format
- ❏ Provides only needed data
- ❏ Includes a key
- ❏ Contains space for the student name, assessor signature, and date completed by self, peer, small group, teacher, or observer
- ❏ Adapts to observations of the individual, partners, small groups, or whole class
- ❏ Can be used to show growth over a period of time
- ❏ Includes space for comments

When multiple observers complete a checklist for one student, compile the checklist results to produce a more complete view of the learner. If appropriate, give the student responsibility for completing the checklist (see Figures 8.11 and 8.12).

Figure 8.11 Class Observation Checklist				

Class/Team _____

Observation Focus _____ Subject _____

Rated by: Teacher _____ Peer _____ Self _____

Date _____ Class _____

Key: O = Outstanding   S = Satisfactory   N = Needs improvement

Student's Name	Standard 1	Standard 2	Standard 3	Standard 4	Comments
1.					
2.					
3.					

Figure 8.12 Oral Report Checklist

Name _____ Date _____

Topic _____

Evaluate all elements with the following key:

O = Outstanding   S = Satisfactory   N = Needs to improve

_____ Accuracy of Information

_____ Quality

_____ Quantity

_____ Organization

_____ Structure of material clear to listener

_____ Details to support the topic

_____ Adequate time, based on relative importance of segments

_____ Presentation

_____ Posture

_____ Voice clarity

_____ Enthusiasm

Comments

Checklist for Independent Work

Teach students how to use the following checklist (Figure 8.13) by sharing the "inner speech" or self-talk needed to respond to each question. Model and practice the use of the checklist before giving it as independent work.

6. Assessment Tools for Reading and Writing

In every subject, it is important to know the student's reading and writing ability level. Success in each content area depends on the learner's skills in understanding passages and in expressing thoughts in written communications. The following assessments provide quick and easy ways to identify the learner's approximate knowledge level in reading and writing (Chapman & King, 2009a).

Figure 8.13		Independent Work Checklist
Yes	No	
☐	☐	I understand the purpose of this assignment.
☐	☐	I know what to do.
☐	☐	I need to ask questions before I begin.
☐	☐	I have the materials I need.
☐	☐	I chose the best place to work.
☐	☐	I have enough work space.
☐	☐	I know the time limit.

Notes

Name _____   Date_____

Oral Reading Assessment

A quick, informal way to check comprehension ability is to read selected passages to the student. Ask the learner to orally rephrase or summarize the passages using the important ideas. A student who cannot comprehend a passage while reading silently usually has a higher level of understanding when reading it aloud.

Check oral reading with statements or questions similar to the following:

1. Name three important facts from your reading.

2. Choose one fact, and tell why it is important.

3. Identify an important event.

4. When did this event occur?

5. Why did this event take place?

6. Summarize the information.

Some students have difficulty with oral reading skills. Provide time for the learners to read the passage independently or with a partner before reading it aloud. This rehearsal time increases an oral reader's confidence and proficiency.

Prompts for Writing

Present the students with a prompt for their writing experience. Choose questions or statements as prompts related to a familiar topic.

Examples

- Write about a favorite time in your life.
- What is the most frightening event you can remember?
- Describe your favorite free-time activity for a friend.
- Describe a character from your favorite book, sitcom, or movie.

Note: If a student has difficulty writing, draw a smiley face on a sticky note. Place the drawing where it is visible. Instruct the learner to talk to the face using each word in the response. The student writes the words as they are spoken. Students usually state information in order, creating organized content when these steps are followed. This is beneficial for the student who can talk about the topic but has trouble writing it.

7. Using Assessment Combinations

Why not create an assessment combination, a collection of items that vary in formats, scales, and indicators? Include checklists, rubrics, Likert scales, comment sections, or open-ended questions. Create instruments that use the best assessment tool to evaluate each item. Teachers often rely on their formal knowledge of well-known rubrics to develop a scale when they are planning a specific assignment. This is a different way of thinking about assessment development. If it is easier to assess a skill or information learned with a checklist than a rubric, use a checklist. Some assessments are more practical in a checklist format.

Design rubrics to accommodate the required assessment results. For example, the four-quadrant rubric may be reduced or expanded to accommodate the individual's specific needs or the task level. Remember that the tool must fit the required criteria and the appropriate indicators. Place information on a checklist if it is a yes or no item.

The goal is to provide the learner with the best instrument to show the most complete assessment picture. Share the selected instrument with students at the beginning of learning to provide a guide for success.

Combined assessments produce efficient tools that make it easy to adapt and differentiate. The content and design of the instrument can be varied for a specific activity, for a group of students, or for an individual learner.

Use novelty in the assessment design. Vary the format and the content to maintain interest and challenge students. For example, if the rubric is usually presented in horizontal boxes, use vertical boxes. Once students know how to use a scale with drawings, use a scale with numbers. When students know how to use a numbered scale successfully, introduce a scale with words. Vary the order of the scales from high to low and low to high so learners realize they must read directions carefully before they begin. Also, be aware that it may take some students longer than others to master a particular scale format. Challenge learners to design their own rubrics, or "rubricate," for self-evaluation during independent assignments and activities. Students benefit tremendously from having the assessment tool in their hands during the introduction of an assignment so they know the specific descriptors of success, as in the following example.

Use the rubric scale, the Likert scale, checklist, and the comment section for assessment (Figure 8.14) while a student is individually engaged in an independent assignment at a center, lab, station, or computer.

Figure 8.14 Assessment of Independent Work

Name _____   Date _____

Working on _____

Rubric

1. Time on task

Little or no time on task	Stays on task with supervision	Stays on task most of the time	Stays on task until task is completed

2. Initial approach

Slow to begin task	Tackles task immediately

3. Works alone

Needs major assistance	Needs some assistance	Works at his or her own pace

Likert Scale

4. Attitude toward working alone

   ←—————————————————————————→

   2   4   6   8

   Negative   Positive

Checklist

5. Check the items that apply.
   _____ a. Understands directions
   _____ b. Asks needed questions
   _____ c. Works independently
   _____ d. Demonstrates appropriate behavior

Comments

_____

_____

_____

_____

(Assessor's) Signature _____   Date _____

8. Design Delights

Have students choose a favorite shape or symbol to identify information learned from the unit or topic of study. Students create the design and write the important points from the study on and around it.

9. Assessing With Journals

To avoid having students approach journal activities with dread, build anticipation for creative journal assignments such as a Double Entry Journal or a Partner Journal (see Figures 8.15, 8.16, and 8.17). Instead of thinking, "Oh no, not journals again!" your students will be eager for their next chance to try an interesting writing experience.

Journaling is a practical, efficient assessment tool. At a glance, you can see when a student uses a skill automatically and correctly, in a journal activity.

Jazzy Journal Assessment

Jazzy Journals make assessment activities interesting and exciting. Challenge students to add their ideas to create Jazzy Journal entries. Consider these suggestions for journal assessment assignments:

- Design a sequence.
- Sketch or draw a picture.
- Create a caricature.
- Use a graphic organizer.
- Make a graffiti list using various fonts and colors.
- Create a song, rap, jingle, rhyme, chant, or cheer.

Use jazzy journal entries to process information. When students use their ideas to create metaphors or similes, they remember facts and concepts, because their brains create visual links and connections.

Use a form similar to the following to create double entry journals. Encourage students to personalize these pages, as time permits, with colors, designs, and various fonts.

Figure 8.15   Double Entry Journal Form

Name _____ Grade _____

Topic _____ Date _____

A. First Notes Date _____	B. Second Notes Date _____

Partners A and B write their ideas about the topic or question in the appropriate column. They take turns writing to assist each other with deeper understanding as they iron out answers to questions or come up with solutions.

Figure 8.16   Partner Journals

Partner A	Partner B

Use a note journal form for students to record important information during various study phases of a specific topic or unit.

Figure 8.17   Note Journal Form

What I Know	Notes From First Reading	Notes From Lecture	Notes to Study

Example

The (fact, concept, standard, skill) is like _____ because _____.

Note: Have student select an item, character, or critter from the list below.

a musical instrument	a type of music	a particular song	a sport
an animal	an athlete	a trip	an event
a piece of furniture	a vehicle	a color	an experience

Encourage students to "jazz up" their journals by using a combination of one or more of the following:

colored yarn	hole-punched dots	neon colors	ribbons
stamps	varied line widths	cut-out shapes	symbols
photos	miniature sketches	pipe cleaners	stars
sayings	magazine clippings	thumbprint drawings	scrapbooking pieces

10. Graphic Organizers

Graphic organizers are visual representations used to record information. Facts and ideas are easier to mentally manipulate, process, and remember when they are applied in a visual way. As learners complete a graphic organizer, they actively engage their thinking as the designs are completed with words or phrases. The visual representation links information in various ways to create personal connections.

Add novelty to students' experiences with graphic organizers to enhance their memory of information. Most students are familiar with numerous font styles found in word processing programs. Encourage the use of different print styles and sizes for specific subtopics or levels of the assess-

> Including graphic organizers on tests would be more creative, challenging, and fun than most traditional objective-style items.
>
> —Burke (2010)

ment tool. For example, record the major topic in a large, bold font with each subtopic in a smaller font. Decreasing various font sizes emphasizes the decreasing value of each subtopic level.

Use graphic organizers to empower learners with realistic assessment tools for meaningful learning experiences. For example, draw an outline of a hand and write on it five facts to remember about a topic, standard, concept, character, or reading selection.

Following a learning segment use pluses, minuses, and intriguing (PMI) organizer (see Figure 8.18) to assess student knowledge, attitude toward the subject material, or a completed product or project. Use this valuable student input to enhance and assess the current and future planning.

Figure 8.18   Pluses, Minuses, and Intriguing (PMI) Charts

Pluses, "+"	Minuses, "−"	Intriguing
I like …	I do not like …	I am still thinking about …
I know …	I do not know …	This reminded me that …
I agree …	I disagree with …	Suggestions
I can use …	I cannot use …	I want to know more about …
Variation:		

Pluses, "+"	Minuses, "−"	Intriguing	Suggestions

11. Prompts for Assessment

A prompt challenges students to assess their learning when an activity is completed. Open-ended statements activate thinking about a specific topic or term. Use the following prompts (as seen in Figure 8.19) as needed:

Figure 8.19   Assessment Prompts

I learned . . .	I was surprised when . . .	I discovered . . .
I still do not understand . . .	I was disappointed in . . .	Next time, I hope we . . .
I will remember . . .	The easiest part was . . .	The best part was . . .
I was pleased that . . .	The hardest part was . . .	The most challenging part was . . .
An interesting part was . . .	I am still thinking about . . .	I need to review . . .
Someone can help me with . . .	I believe . . .	I am sure about. . .
I wonder if . . .	One solution is . . .	I can explain . . .
This reminds me of . . .	I can apply this . . .	I predict . . .

12. Assessing With a Blank Page

Often a learner says, "I studied so hard for this test, but I studied the wrong things!" This individual feels time was wasted because the responses did not demonstrate what was learned about the new topic. To eliminate this problem, add a blank page to the test, and give the student an opportunity to write information he or she knows about the topic. Provide the blank-page assessment as an option, not as a mandate. Do not remove points if the test-taker has incorrect entries or makes no additions to the blank page.

This novel idea helps the teacher learn information the student knows. Give extra points when the student correctly extends a response or states information not addressed on the test. Consider giving the student one point for each correct fact added to the test score. If the student adds ten correct facts or ideas to an already perfect score, the score becomes 110 points. Give praise or extra points for accurate responses. This is an exciting way for students to show what they know. Adding a blank page to the end of a test motivates students to study and prepare for the assessment.

13. Performance Assessment

The teacher becomes a Wondering Wizard when unveiling a learner's thinking. Discuss the wonders of the brain and the fact that every mind solves problems in different ways. Teachers are like wizards because they know how, when, and where to present quality assignments to match the learning and stimulate thinking. The teacher as a Wondering Wizard gives students opportunities to show what they know in creative ways as seen in the following chart (see Figure 8.20).

Figure 8.20 Performance Assessments

Show it musically.	Explain it.	Demonstrate it.	Write it.	Show it visually.
Create a musical.	Debate it.	Create an exhibit.	Write a story.	Illustrate it.
Put it to a beat.	Make a speech.	Use manipulatives to explain it.	Make a list.	Create a poster gallery.
Sing it.	Apply to another situation.	Act it out.	Construct and conduct a survey.	Develop a PowerPoint presentation.
Rap it.	Complete a detailed summary.	Compare/Contrast it.	Write an editorial.	Create a replica.
Create a rhythmic pattern.	Write a critique.	Show it on a graphic organizer.	Write it on a chart.	Recreate scenes or events.
Write a poem.	Defend the data.	Make a timeline with illustrations.	Log it.	Create a caricature
Create a jingle.	Put it in simpler words.	Gather and share evidence on mini posters.	Write from a character's point of view.	Construct an exhibit.
Engage in a choral reading.	Describe the step-by-step process.	Create a flipbook with drawings	Plead a case. Record statements.	Create a book jacket.
Chant it	Make graphs to create a presentation.	Make a display of the characters.	Write a news flash.	Design a cartoon strip.
Write and perform a cheer.	Make a journal entry to sequence the process.	Design a hands-on bulletin board.	Write a research paper.	Make a diorama.
Create sounds for the setting.	Use color-coding to identify steps.	Develop a sequenced plan.	Plot it on a graphic organizer.	Create a brochure.

14. Teacher-Made Tests

The most effective tests are made by the teacher for individuals in a class. Be cautious about using the same tests for each class and year after year. Standards, units, and students change. Customize instructional plans for the current assessment results and needs of individuals and the group. Design teacher-made tests to differentiate assessment with tools and strategies thoughtfully tailored for learners.

What Does an Effective Teacher-Made Test Show?

Design teacher-made tests to reveal the following:

- The amount of information learned
- The student's strengths and needs
- The skills or concepts the learner needs next
- Misconceptions requiring interventions or more background information
- How the student is processing information
- The learner's interpretations

Use a Checklist to Analyze the Value of the Teacher-Made Test

☐ Does the test show what the student knows?

☐ Will the learner be able to use this test format?

☐ When is the most effective time for this test?

☐ Can the test be used as a pretest and a posttest?

☐ Is it better to use this assessment at the end as a summative evaluation of the information learned?

☐ Does the student need to know this information or skill as a key link or step for past or future learning?

☐ Are the students prepared for the test?

☐ Is the tested information needed for lifelong learning?

☐ Has the student demonstrated that he or she knows the information in other ways, such as telling or demonstrating it?

☐ What test format is needed for this learner?

☐ Is appropriate time allowed for quality student responses?

☐ Is each question clearly stated?

☐ Are the directions easy to follow?

☐ How will the test be scored or graded?

☐ Do some sections of the instrument need to be worth more points than other sections?

Format Options for Teacher-Made Tests

Students learn how to follow detailed directions when they are presented with a variety of assessment formats. Explain how to approach each testing format when it is introduced. Periodically review the procedures. Model your thinking for each approach by verbalizing your thoughts, or self-talk. This shows students how to use their metacognitive skills. Also, lead conversations and share tips showing students how to work with the various assessment formats.

True/False

Remember that students have a 50 percent chance to answer "true or false" questions correctly. Guessing plays a vital role in addressing this assessment format. True/false questions are easy to grade.

Multiple Choice

Teach students the following tips and strategies to approach and process multiple-choice problems.

- If you know the answer, mark it. Do not second guess yourself.
- It is usually easy to narrow the responses to two possible, correct answers.

    1. Explain *why* the least obvious answers do not work.

    2. Explain why it is easy to eliminate an *incorrect* answer.

    3. Select the correct answer.

- Work with game formats and practice how to approach multiple-choice questions. Explain some of the key secret clues of getting to the right answer using the following tips.
    - Guess if you do not know the answer at all.
    - Do not spend too long on one question. Mark it to revisit. Move on and come back.
    - Usually the choices that include the words *always*, *never*, or *none* can be eliminated as the answer.
    - Look for key words and phrases.
    - If there is an "all of the above" option, it is often the answer.

Fill in the Blank

Students recall facts and details from the information and record their answers. Fill-in-the-blank tests may include two or three words presented for answer selection or a word bank. Sometimes learners may have the option for using an open book or their notes to fill in the blanks. Include examples in daily class and homework assignments for practice opportunities. The following are examples of fill-in-the-blank, short-answer questions:

- The definition of the word *hibernation* is _____.
- The _____, _____, and _____ are the three branches of government.

Open-Ended Questions

Open-ended questions or statements give students opportunities to respond in detail using their own words. These are often called discussion questions. Present the criteria for grading on the test. Try this variation! Provide several open-ended questions for student choice or selection.

Examples

- Explain the steps in a long division problem.
- How do cells divide?

Performance Tests

A performance test involves hands-on experiences or demonstrations designed to show the learner's ability and prove understanding, such as a lab experiment or a simulation. It may involve an ongoing activity to show what the student knows, or it may conclude with a one-time performance. For example, the student may show where Egypt is located on the map or move the hands on a clock to reflect a specific time. The learner may use manipulatives to demonstrate a solution to a problem. Refer to the Wondering Wizard chart in this chapter (Figure 8.20) for a hodgepodge of performance assessment ideas.

Skills Test

This type of test gives the student an opportunity to perform skills in a demonstration. Examples of skills tests include making a birdhouse in the woodworking shop, serving a volleyball in physical education, or applying a specific skill in a computer program.

Problem-Based Assessment

The problem-based assessment uses a real-life situation or problem. The learner produces reports, artifacts, and collections as data. An essential question, or hypothesis, is often chosen to investigate a local, state, national, or global problem of interest to students.

15. Portfolios

The word *portfolio* is derived from the Latin word *portare*, which means "to carry," and folio, which refers to "a leaf or sheet of paper." The term *portfolio* is common in the art and business world, where it refers to a case that holds artwork, sheets of paper, official documents, or artifacts.

In the classroom, teachers and students use portfolios of various sizes, shapes, and forms to collect and organize work samples. Guide students as they individually assume responsibility for completing and gathering work samples and other entries for their portfolios.

Portfolio Assessment

In portfolio assessment, the collected work samples can be used by students, teachers, and parents to monitor progress. The major purpose of portfolio assessment is to engage students in the evaluation and identification of their needs and strengths to show growth and progress.

The needs and strengths of learners can be showcased in their individual portfolio collections. This information provides assessment data to evaluate and guide their instruction. Analysis of a student's work samples provides data that reflect understanding of a particular standard or skill. The teacher uses the information to target gaps in learning so the student receives the needed next steps in instruction. The information derived through portfolio assessment becomes a vital tool to guide planning.

Design portfolio assessment to do the following:

- Showcase work samples
- Empower learners
- Show stages of progress and performance
- Demonstrate evidence of accomplishments
- Improve self-efficacy, the "I can do" feeling
- Teach students to be self-reflective
- Provide avenues for self-analysis and self-improvement
- Guide students to higher levels of thinking through self-evaluation and peer critiques
- Generate genuine pride in accomplishments
- Provide evidence to support grades
- Reveal needs for interventions
- Create a Showcase for Success

What Can Be Used as a Portfolio?

Keep in mind that the major purpose of the portfolio is to gather work samples that reflect the student's best work and needs. If a portfolio assessment activity is planned more than one time during the year, vary the collection tools, the collection process, and the presentation style. Adapt the examples in Figure 8.21 to create novel containers for portfolio assessment experiences.

Portfolio Briefs

The word *brief* is derived from the Latin word *breve*, which means "summary." When the term *brief* refers to important documents, it means "a condensed version that includes major facts or points."

A shorter version of the traditional portfolio, a portfolio brief, adds novelty to assignments. The portfolio brief contains student-selected highlights from work samples.

Figure 8.21 Portfolio Options

Collection Devices	Cover Designs	Page Layout	Gathering Process	Presentation Style
• Folder • Case • Crate • Notebook • Box • X-ray folder • Large envelope • Poster board (folded or stapled) • Website • Thumb drive	• Topic symbols • Personal interests and hobbies • Graffiti • Geometric shapes • Scrapbook ideas • Photos • Drawings • Home page on website	• Frames • Collages • Illustrations • Examples • Scrapbooking ideas • Transparency sleeve • Photo album • PowerPoint presentation	• 3 to 4 examples • Selected passages • Highlights • Summaries • Display or exhibit • Web • Interview • Research • Independent practice • Photos	• Oral report • Interview • Conference • Conversation • Circles • Family night • Slide presentation with narration • Talk show • Documentary • Booklet • Diary • Journal

In other words, it is a sample of a sample. Each entry contains a succinct or concise view of a student's strengths and needs. This work collection technique has advantages over the traditional portfolio because the amount of time needed for data analysis is greatly reduced. A large amount of time that the teacher and the student usually spend sifting through numerous, detailed activities and work samples are eliminated.

The teacher and students may need to use this to develop new, innovative ways to create portfolio briefs. In a traditional portfolio, students place numerous pages that reflect their abilities. The portfolio brief challenges the student to select samples as highlights of the best work. Each entry in the portfolio becomes a snapshot of the learner's ability. The selection process teaches students to assess their daily work and leads to self-directed learning.

Examples

My best work is _____.

I need help with _____.

Sample writing assignments for portfolio brief entries include the following:

- Choose the best paragraph from your essay, and paste it at the top of a piece of paper. Rate your work on a scale from 2 through 10. Write two sentences describing how to improve your work.
- In 25 to 30 words, describe the most important person or event in our lesson today.
- List five important facts from today's lesson.
- Write a word problem illustrating the math procedure we learned today.
- Complete the last five problems.

- Retell the information through two thumbprint or stick characters.

- Retell the passage, and write it in your own words. Create a design using one or more symbols repeatedly around the writing to create a frame.

- What will happen next? Draw stick figures with speech bubbles to illustrate your thoughts.

Portfolio Brief-Preparation Center

Adapt the following materials and supplies for the portfolio brief center.

scissors   hole punch   stapler   highlighters   markers   glue

glitter pens   colored pencils   paper clips   wallpaper scraps   stickers

construction paper   paper in neon colors and designs

Showcase Scoring

Students and teachers develop a scoring rubric for the portfolio assessment, such as the following example:

5. Above and Beyond

- Completed more activities than required
- All work complete and organized
- Turned everything in on time

4. On Track

- All assignments complete
- Organized work
- Completed on time

3. Not Quite There

- Missing one or two pieces
- Not well organized
- One day late

2. Thrown Together

- Three or more pieces missing
- No evidence of organization
- Two days late

1. A "No Show" Effort

- Did not try
- No examples of ability
- More than two days late

Comment Box

Teacher:

Student:

SUMMARY

Select appropriate assessment tools to use at the end of the learning to discover the student's insights, progress with skills, and knowledge level. The data represent what the learner knows at the current point in time. The information guides planning for the next unit or topic of study.

> If students and teachers use tests as exciting, engaging challenges to show what was learned, we predict higher test scores and more rewarding learning experiences.
>
> —Chapman and King
> (2009a, p. 5)

Give students opportunities to apply the mastered skills in new ways for practice and review. Use novelty to teach the skills that are not mastered by planning customized approaches to incorporate the learners' intelligences and learning styles. Share the results and plans with the students.

As a unit of study or lesson segment comes to conclusion, identify the strategies and activities that made your learners successful. Abandon the techniques that did not work for you. Explore new ways to meet your learners' needs. This approach presents formative assessment after the learning as an ongoing adventure that creates new discoveries for you and your students.

DIFFERENTIATING SUMMATIVE ASSESSMENTS 9

Essential Question: How can the diverse needs of learners be accommodated during formal assessments?

Prepare learners for assessment using a variety of instructional strategies to match the many ways they learn. Consider the learner's physical, emotional, and academic needs in planning each assessment experience. Keep the learners informed abut the purpose, format, and each aspect of the assessment process to alleviate anxiety and frustration.

HOW CAN STANDARDIZED ASSESSMENTS BE DIFFERENTIATED?

Standardized assessments contain specific guidelines and directions in the teacher's manual. These formal assessments contain specific requirements. The district or school administrator may establish additional guidelines or procedures.

The standardized assessment guidelines and directives from the district and school-site administrators must be followed. Fortunately, there are several aspects of standardized assessments that have no restrictions. This autonomy gives the teacher opportunities to differentiate assessment. Preparations are made to implement the mandated regulations. Look for ways to differentiate in areas that enhance the individual student's opportunities to succeed.

Each learner approaches tests with different attitudes, skills, and expectations for success. Standardized assessments, however, are administered with the same directions, time limits, response formats, and questions. There is little reference to the diverse ways students learn and perform in the classroom.

Accommodations: In the Teacher's Hands

It is not possible to accommodate all learners during standardized tests because of formal procedures and guidelines. These rules and regulations are out of the teacher's hands, or realm of control. Thoroughly review the directions that accompany an assessment before considering student accommodations. Identify the specific factors that are *out* of the teacher's hands. List the factors related to the assessment experience that are *in* the teacher's control. These factors may be adjusted to accommodate individual needs (Chapman & King, 2009c).

Use the following suggestions and tips to differentiate for individual students during assessment experiences. Implement changes in routine practice sessions throughout the year so students become comfortable with them. For example, move the desks apart, and make accommodations during chapter and unit tests.

Seating

- Provide opportunities for students to choose comfortable places to work.
- Make a specific seating assignment to meet an individual's need.
- Space the desks to allow free movement for monitoring.

Time

- If possible, decide how many tests to administer each day, and select the most appropriate time to give them.
- Plan brief transition sessions of enjoyable, physical activity in fresh air to rejuvenate the students' brains. If it is not possible to go outside between assessment segments, engage the learners in challenging but relaxing activities in high-interest areas.
- If possible, administer assessment when the students are most alert. For example, research reveals that high school students are most alert in the afternoon.

Tools

- Provide the tools the student needs to be successful if they fit within the assessment rules and guidelines. For example, a student's comprehension may improve if allowed to use a reading guide, such as an index card, ruler, or marker while taking a test.
- Make scratch paper, calculators, pencils, placeholders, pencil grips, and erasers available.
- Refer to #2 test-taking pencils throughout the year as "smart pencils."
- Use novel tools to entice the student during assessment sessions.

Personal Needs

- Provide a privacy cubicle to a student who is easily distracted.
- Separate students who are peer-dependent.
- Identify learners who have special needs that require specific equipment, and have it available for the assessment session.

CREATE A POSITIVE TESTING ENVIRONMENT

Teachers, administrators, and parents prepare and encourage students to do their best on tests. At the same time they may unintentionally create barriers to the students' success by developing test-taking fears and anxieties. The emphasis on test results places more pressure on everyone associated with the school. In turn, the drive for higher test scores places more pressure on learners.

> We believe everyone should view tests as celebrations of the brain's phenomenal abilities, not as dreaded events.
>
> —Chapman &
> King (2009, p. xi)

Brain research and common sense tells us that the brain functions best when in a relaxed, non-threatened state. The brain cannot devote its total thinking capacity to benefit the student when it is coping with fear of failure, anxiety, and stress.

Identify words or phrases used by educators, students, and parents that have negative connotations for assessment. Add to the list throughout the year. Be aware of negative comments, activities, or actions in the school and home that create barriers to test success. Develop specific plans to create a positive testing environment that leads each student to view assessments as valuable experiences that will expedite the learning journey.

GIVE EFFECTIVE DIRECTIONS

It is not uncommon to complete assessment instructions and immediately see a student with his or her hand raised to ask the frustrating question, "Now what am I supposed to do?" Why does this happen?

Use the following tip to keep this from occurring. Remember to get the students established in the selected seating arrangement and supply them with the needed materials for the task. Give directions immediately before students are to carry them out. Also, remember to make the directions as short and clear as possible. It may be necessary to give one or two steps at a time for a procedure. This improves comprehension, clarifies the message, and paces tasks. Ask various students to repeat the directions so misunderstanding can be avoided. This strategy works with directions for any assignment.

Standardized test guidelines usually require that the test directions be read exactly as printed. If so, read in a clear, distinct, friendly voice with verbal emphasis on important directional information. If possible, review the directions in advance, and practice reading them.

Direction Variations

When giving assessments, it is important that directions are clearly understood. They should be purposeful and fully explained, so the students can carry them out with ease and correctness. Throughout the year, vary formative assessment directions to provide students with practice in working with the same information in different ways. When directions are varied, students who have difficulty with one approach have opportunities to respond to the information in another way.

TEACH TEST-TAKING SKILLS

Analyze the demands of tests, and determine how to embed the test-taking skills in motivating classroom activities. Students need to be taught, practice, and master these specific skills throughout the school year.

Self-Regulated Skills Needed for Test Success

Teach learners to use self-regulation skills during tests. Remind them to keep their mental wheels turning and on the right track. Share the following tips in assessment sessions.

- Control your thinking.
- Listen for key words.
- Ask needed questions before the assessment.
- Concentrate on the task.
- Monitor your time, so you can pace the work.
- Do your best.
- Show what you know!
- Review your answers.

Stumped and Stalled

Show learners how to use strategies similar to the following when they have difficulty with a test item or when they don't know the answer to a question.

- Look for clues.
- Visualize yourself as you were learning this information.
- Reword or simplify the directions.
- Chunk it! Place the information in a category or group.
- Compare or contrast it with a familiar object or person.
- Read the directions without the unknown word.
- Replace the unknown word with a familiar word.

Breakthrough Clues for Reading Directions

Teach students to look for breakthrough clues in the test directions if they have difficulty understanding what to do. Use the following activities to read directions.

Be a Spy for Words That Qualify

A qualifying word intensifies, modifies, or limits the meaning of another word or phrase. Emphasize the importance of being a spy for words that qualify, because they can change the meaning of a statement or question.

always	all	never	none	only	true	false
except	more than	less than	some	negative	many	positive

Note the Negatives

Prefixes change or modify the meaning of words. Teach students to be aware of the prefixes that create a negative word or phrase in the test directions.

un	non	in	il	dis	im	ir	a	ex

Check, Check, Check

Rehearse the following self-talk questions until students automatically use them during tests.

- Is my work legible?
- Did I copy the information correctly on the answer sheet?
- Does my answer make sense?
- Are my answer spaces correctly marked or filled in?
- Do I need to erase unnecessary marks?

GRADING

Whole books can be and have been written about grading. It is a controversial and emotional topic in many ways. Here are some helpful grading guidelines to differentiate learning and assessment. Give students a combination of informal and formal grades. Use the results from the assignments that reveal the student's knowledge base and some assignments based on his or her ability level. Grades recorded on report cards represent the student's academic progress and grade-level standards related to the subject.

Behavior, effort, and attitude are not indicators of ability and performance. Of course, these factors influence learning and may accompany the academic report, but they need to appear in a separate section or form.

There will always be subjectivity in grades. Gather as much solid evidence as possible, and give the grade that reflects the evidence.

The Final Grade

Obtain some grades from the student's work when he or she is performing at his or her knowledge base level. For students working with intervention assignment

> In the differentiated classroom, there must be a combination of assessments so that a true picture of the student's performance is given in the final grade.
>
> —Chapman & King (2009a, p. 191)

below grade level, these grades will be high, because the student understands and is ready for this information. Add grades from his or her work on independent assignments that are on the same level as other class members. For many students, this will bring the grade down because they do not perform as well on grade-level work. In other words, provide some grades based on the student's readiness level and some grades on grade level to provide an overall, unbiased view of the learner.

These grades reflect the student's current level of work as well as the expectation level. This grading process is fair because it reveals a true picture of the student's performance in relation to the standards at that grade level.

Parent Conferencing to Report Assessment

Plan a parent conference to gain their support as partners in the student's education program. Remember many parents are intimidated by teachers. Create a cordial atmosphere. Let the parents know that they are major contributors to their student's success.

Use the following sandwich technique to introduce weak areas as indicated by the assessment data. Begin the session with praise for the student, and then approach the area of need with a clear, concise description and work samples. Make detailed suggestions for improvement. Close the session with genuine praise for the student. This approach sandwiches negative comments between two or more positive statements. Give the parents specific suggestions to assist, encourage, and support the learner to foster academic success.

Use the following guidelines to organize conference procedures:

1. Carefully review the data gathered, especially your student's portfolio and the observation notes.

2. Begin the conference with a focus on two to three of the student's academic and personal strengths.

3. Avoid reviewing past negative behaviors unless they continue to influence current performance.

4. Identify and discuss the learner's areas of need.

5. Provide specific examples of activities to practice at home.

6. End the conference with positive comments.

7. Remind parents to use the student's favorite ways to learn to strengthen his or her weaker areas.

Examples

- If the student enjoys artwork, encourage the learner to create illustrations for skills or concepts.

- If the student enjoys movement activities, encourage the learner to act out the skill or concept.

8. Emphasize the emotional barriers to academic success created by negative comments and actions.

9. Encourage parents to use specific positive comments that support and motivate the learner.

10. Praise the parents for taking their valuable time to participate in the conference.

SUMMARY

In this age of accountability, we must always remember that the goal of assessment is to identify ways to assist individual learners. Students should know that each formative assessment activity is designed to gather information for their improvement.

> The wealth of knowledge acquired by students should be celebrated as a bright point in their educational experiences: too often, though, standardized tests place a dark cloud over the joy of learning. This doesn't have to be true. An appropriately staged test scene creates positive attitudes and successful experiences to foster the love of learning.
>
> —Chapman & King (2009c, p. 4)

ASSESSMENT FOR DIFFERENTIATED INSTRUCTION AND FLEXIBLE GROUPING 10

Essential Question: How can we incorporate effective formative assessments within the strategies and activities frequently used to differentiate instruction with flexible grouping?

A major goal of differentiated assessment is to diagnose individual learners using appropriate tools and flexible grouping. Whenever possible, select or design assessment activities to create positive attitudes toward assessment. Intriguing, challenging tools motivate learners to reveal information stored in memory. Students can actively engage in removing mental blocks and negative feelings in strategically devised formative assessments.

The instructional strategies examined in this chapter include using technology, cubing, choice boards, and agendas. Ideas are presented for establishing stations and learning zones. Adapt the tips, techniques, and suggestions to your students' assessment needs. Use the flexible grouping scenarios and designs for effective formative assessment and personalized planning.

USING TECHNOLOGY FOR ASSESSMENT

Technology enhances assessment for teaching and learning. It must be planned strategically and appropriately. A drawback to using technology is relying on it as a time filler or killer. Make each interaction with assessment technology rewarding and productive. It is an effective assessment tool to use before, during, and after the learning. The experiences can be designed for the total class, individuals working alone, with a partner, or in a small groups.

Technology Software

Become familiar with software options to assist in quality assessment planning. Some software is purchased or received as "freebies" with adopted series and packages. Examine each resource thoroughly to be sure it fits the needs of the students and the assessed standards. Also rate each segment carefully for boredom or excitement.

If it is boring or does not meet the required needs, do not use it. Be aware of blanket use for materials that are not designed for your learners.

For example, some companies have a pre-post test for each unit or chapter. It was written from a global perspective and often will not correlate with your standards. Use these suggestions to make the pre-post test a productive assessment.

- Read each item, and eliminate the ones that do not address the identified standards, concepts, and skills. Tell students to skip these items.
- If you can unlock the program, rearrange the questions to better accommodate your students.
- Mix easy and difficult items.
- Design your own test if it does not fit your students' needs.

Performance Assessment Using Technology

In performance assessments, learners create products to demonstrate what they know. Technology provides the learners with enticing, alluring assessments. The following examples can be used as independent or small-group assignments to differentiate assessment activities. They can be designed for an assessment choice board and displayed in the room.

- Demonstrate with an interactive whiteboard.
- Develop a PowerPoint presentation.
- Design a webpage.
- Produce a podcast.
- Organize a blog forum.
- Create an instructional game.
- Create a video.

Assess with technology when the following occurs:

- The tool matches the information.
- It is relevant.
- It accommodates learners.
- It provides constructive data for immediate results and feedback.
- The tool provides the most effective way to demonstrate knowledge.
- An alternative assessment is needed.
- The student has received thorough instructions for using the tool.
- The student knows how to use the technology with little or no assistance.
- The data gathered can be used to customize instructional plans.

Technology-Based Assessment Tools

The market is saturated with exciting tools to use for assessment. Add to the following list of technology-based assessment tools.

Digital portfolio	Camcorder	Audio recorder
Scanner	Digital camera	Flip video camera
Clicker response system	Interactive board	Laptop

Technology is becoming a vital tool in teaching and learning with an important role in assessment. These tools are used to monitor individual progress and keep anecdotal records while recording and sharing test data. Other benefits include communicating with parents and students through e-mail, blogs, school websites, and forums. Teachers can post lesson plans, interventions, homework, assessment results, and announcements to maintain open lines of communication. Stay abreast of the latest equipment, terminology, gadgets, research, programs, and innovative technological advances to enhance assessment experiences.

ASSESSMENT CUBING

Cubing activities offer students assessment choices and add novelty to thinking. Create cubes by covering boxes, pieces of foam, or cube-shaped containers. Another way to create a cubing activity is to write six items on a flat surface as in Figure 10.1.

1. Choose words from the domain of thinking on Bloom's Taxonomy, and place one term in each section on the cube as in the following example. Customize the terms to assess the student on his or her level of thinking in a specific subject. Select a character, place, event, topic, item, term, or any noun as the game topic.

2. The student selects a side of the cube to complete by using a die, spinner, or secret number.

3. Each player reports about the noun using the term by his or her lucky number.

Figure 10.1 Assessment Cubing Example

I. Propose	2. Demonstrate
3. Rate	4. Describe
5. Predict	6. Define

Variations for Assessment Cubing Activities

- Select six terms to fit the concept, topic, vocabulary word, or artifact in a study.

- Choose an object, and place terms on the cube to describe it. This can be a written or oral activity, depending on the student's needs.

- Collectively choose one object to discuss with each of the selected cubing terms.

- Use cubing activities in a station. Students draw or write about a topic, vocabulary word, or concept using the terms.

- Roll a die, and use the term on the cube with the matching number to apply to the object, word, or concept. If two students roll the same number, they apply the word in different ways.

- Design cubes with a different assessment activity for a specific topic on each side. The learner rolls the cube to select the task.

CHOICE BOARDS

An assessment choice board presents various ways for learners to demonstrate their understanding and current knowledge. The choice board can assess information of a learning segment such as a standard, skill, lesson, chapter, unit, or grading period. Each assessment on the choice board is specifically designed to meet students' identified needs, abilities, and interests.

Choice develops confidence, fosters independence, creates a sense of responsibility, and gives students ownership in learning. Choice boards motivate students because they provide opportunities for students to select the assessment activities. The boards give teachers flexible tools to create assessment assignments for all subject areas and skills.

Designing Choice Boards

Prior to designing a choice board, consider how much experience learners have in making choices. If students have had few or no opportunities to make selection decisions, begin with two choices.

Examples

- Use a four-square outline to create four choices.
- Use a tic-tac-toe outline to create nine choices.
- Use a bingo board outline to create twenty-five choices.

Adding Novelty

To add novelty to choice boards, use topic or seasonal shapes, outlines, or unique designs as the background for the choice board selections. Try these shapes and outlines or create your own!

wheel	hand shape	pizza	rainbow
rocket	pyramid	flag	open book
tree	clouds	scrolls	seasonal items

One of the most effective choice boards is designed with the students' input by brainstorming ideas. This is an enticing way for students to learn many self-assessment strategies and practice using them. Use the following guidelines to create quality choice boards for assessment experiences:

1. Select a place in the lesson plans where the criteria and the assessments are appropriate for choice board use.

2. Brainstorm an extensive list of assessment choice activities.

3. Place a check mark beside activities on the list that meet the student's assessment needs for the learning standard.

4. Count the number of check marks.

5. Draw a choice board using a shape to fit the number of selected activities. For example, use five petals on a flower for activities or tentacles of an octopus for eight choices.

6. Place each selected activity on a section of the choice board.

7. Number each choice.

Variation: Use a wild card as an option. When the wild card is selected, the student creates an assessment tool or strategy with teacher approval.

Using Choice Boards Wisely

Choice boards are flexible assessment tools. The following list contains various ways to present the tasks:

- Base the assignment on the winning strategy for a tic-tac-toe or bingo game. For example, use this direction: Complete a horizontal, vertical, or diagonal row of activities.

- Place assessment activities for the novice learner in the even-numbered sections. Use the odd-numbered sections for assessment activities designed to challenge students who have a high degree of mastery.

- Create assignments that give students opportunities to use a random selection process. For example, use this direction: Select three activities from the choice board to complete.

- Assign specific items that meet the learner's needs. Consider the following examples:
  - Complete the bottom row of assessment activities on the choice board.
  - Complete the activities in the four corners.

- Place a letter, such as A, B, C, D, above each column, and number the rows 1, 2, 3, 4. Strategically place specific assessment activities to accommodate individual or group needs. For example, complete A4, C2, D3, and an activity of your choice.
- Use a crucial skill in the wild card space, and make it a requirement for the assignment. Consider the following examples:
  ○ Everyone must complete a row that includes the wild card.
  ○ Complete the activity in the wild card space and two activities of your choice.

Note: Give the student opportunities to design and select the choice board assessment activities whenever possible.

Liz Bennett, an educational consultant and trainer, reminds teachers to avoid giving choices at the expense of learning. Students naturally make choices that match their strongest learning styles, intelligences, and interests. When choices are given in all situations, "their strengths become stronger, and their weaknesses become weaker." Use collected knowledge of students and sound planning strategies to decide when choice assessment activities are valuable experiences.

Figure 10.2 presents innovative ways for students to show what they learned from a text passage, a specific reading selection, a unit, or a subject. Students may be given a rubric or checklist for the assessment activities so they know the criteria and descriptors of success.

Figure 10.2 Assessment Choice Board		
Topic _____		
1. Use an Idea Tree to show the causes and effects of _____.	2. Plot the information you learned about your favorite character on a stick figure.	3. Compare and contrast the two events on a Venn diagram.
4. Use a concept map to organize the important details.	5. Design a sequence chart for important events.	6. Place five important facts on a Hand Organizer.

Challenge students by giving them opportunities to design assessment strategies and tools for the choice board. When students know how to create assessment activities, they can apply this strategy as a self-assessment tool during independent work.

Self-selection gives learners a voice in the assessment process. Students enjoy choosing activities that allow them to apply information in different ways to show what they know.

ASSESSMENT AGENDAS

Agendas are specific assignments strategically planned to meet the needs of an individual or a small group. Agendas are occasionally referred to as menus. They are implemented to manage work time when individuals or small groups of students need experiences with different skills, topics, concepts, interests, information, or strategies. A student(s) works with the agenda while other group members work on a different lesson or activity.

The teacher explains the list of activities in the agenda assignment and sets the deadline. The agenda may include opportunities for student choice, such as selection of activities, the order of completion, or the pacing for each item. The assignments are placed in a folder, chart, or a specified area. View Figure 10.3 for a sample agenda. The student is able to work independently with the detailed, outlined assignments and tasks designed for his or her readiness level.

The agenda items can be checked or routinely assessed to create a work log. As learners engage in regular assessments, they become aware of their needs, rates of progress, and success.

Figure 10.3   Agenda Assessment

Student _____   Date _____

❐ Go on a scavenger hunt and locate ____ facts about ____. Place a sticky note to flag each discovered fact. Write details about each fact on the sticky note.

❐ Make a collage about what you learned from the _____.

❐ Complete five out of the ten story problems in the computer program ____.

❐ Choose two activities to complete from the assessment choice board.

Due _____

Student's Signature _____

Teacher's Signature _____

Reflections, Comments, and Suggestions

_____

_____

_____

_____

Assess the Agenda Plan

Use the following list to assess the agenda plan.

A quality assessment agenda allows the learner to do the following:

____ 1. Work with the needed standard and content.

____ 2. Show evidence of acquired knowledge.

____ 3. Feel challenged.

____ 4. Work at an appropriate pace.

____ 5. Choose the order for working with the tasks.

___ 6. Develop independence.

___ 7. Manage personal time.

___ 8. Work at his or her readiness level.

___ 9. Include a reflective assessment activity.

STATIONS, CENTERS, AND LEARNING ZONES FOR ASSESSMENT

Use a variety of stations, labs, or centers for focused assessments that provide challenges with manipulatives and opportunities to create products. The best time to assess the learner's ability and knowledge is when the individual is actively engaged at his or her own pace (Chapman & King, 2008).

Exploratory Stations

An Exploratory Station is an excellent place to assess the learners' performance experiences. Provide materials and set the rules. Students use the provided items to discover, invent, create, and process using their chosen learning styles. Assess by asking appropriate questions to analyze their thinking processes and provide opportunities for them to explain their actions and interpret how or why something happened. Use the responses to determine what needs to happen next for students. Design Exploratory Stations for learners to investigate topics in subject areas.

Adapt the following guidelines and rules for an Exploratory Station:

- Only use the items provided in the station.
- Work in the appropriate space.
- Respect others.
- Use materials wisely.
- Display the product in the designated area.
- Organize and clean the work area before leaving it.

Assessment for Exploratory Stations

- The learner stayed on task.
- This station is a wise use of time.
- These activities promote thinking and investigation.
- Materials are appropriate, available, and accessible.
- The participant's mind is challenged in a novel way.

Structured Stations

Structured Stations may be designed for a specific topic or skill in any subject. The tasks and procedures are established for students to follow. The appropriate materials are provided, and the rules are set. Adapt the following guidelines to outline tasks, present rules, and select materials for the Structured Station Assessment Activity.

Structured Station Assignment

1. Create a model to teach the information you learned.

2. Place the model on a piece of construction paper.

3. Write your name on or near the model in a visible space.

4. Display your work in the designated space.

Rules

- Use the materials provided.

- Follow and complete the directions.

- Work in the appropriate space.

- Clean up the station and work area before you leave.

- Journal your problems and successes at the station today.

Assess the Structured Station

When setting up and implementing a Structured Station, assess it with the following checklist:

_____ Objectives and goals are identified.

_____ Directions and procedures are clear and concise.

_____ Tasks are defined and easy to follow.

_____ Activities can be completed without supervision.

_____ Materials are available and accessible.

_____ Time is used wisely.

Assessment Station Management Tips

Assessment stations are usually assigned by the teacher. Whenever possible, provide opportunities for students to choose where and how they complete the tasks including working independently or with a partner.

Create signs and labels so students know the location of materials or workstations. If the classroom is not conducive to movement, permit students to create a special workspace around their desks. Valuable stations can be created with materials stored in plastic bags, folders, or boxes. Post the station's name, rules, directions, and procedures in a visible space with the materials.

Stations are not intended for busywork or for wasting time. If a station is not working or the students are not following the rules, close the station. Keep the station open when it is a productive place. It is fun and practical to design temporary open and closed signs for the stations.

Examples

Closed for Repair	Open for Business	Open
Grand Opening	Site Under Reconstruction	Closed

Assessing Station Time

The most productive aspect of station time assessment is its ability to provide data on how a student processes and interprets his or her thinking during tasks. It also provides information to identify individual weaknesses and strengths in specific areas. The purpose of workstation time is to record key observations that provide insights into what the student knows. Record, interpret, and use the formative assessment data to plan differentiated instruction.

Questioning for Station Time

Use open-ended questions to probe the learner's mind and extend thinking. Use questions similar to the following:

- Tell me what you are doing.
- How did you _____?
- Tell me more about this.
- Why did you use _____?

ASSESSMENT FOR FLEXIBLE GROUPING

Flexible grouping strategies accommodate the learner's needs for instruction or assessment. The acronym TAPS represents four basic ways to design assessment groups:

T = Total Group   **A** = Alone   **P** = Partners   **S** = Small Groups

Total Group	The entire class is assessed as work is completed. The same directions and expectations are set for everyone.
Alone	Each student works independently on a specific assessment task.
Partners	Two students are assessed as they work together on an open-ended question, a brainstorming activity, a discussion topic, a project, or a presentation.
Small Groups	Four to six students work on an assessment task. Each group member is accountable for his or her own learning. Individual strengths and talents shine during challenging, cooperative assignments and discussions as students learn from each other.

Grouping Decisions

The teacher decides if it is best for the student to work independently, with a partner, in a small group, or with the total group. The following questionnaire is designed to assess optimal grouping designs before, during, and after learning. Consider the advantages and disadvantages of each grouping scenario. Analyze the responses to determine the effectiveness of the strategy. Remember to use flexible grouping to meet specific student needs.

T for Total Group

Assessing Before Teaching

- Which lesson segments do I need to teach to the total class?
- What is this class's overall state of readiness for this material and these concepts?
- Are appropriate visuals, props, graphics, and other materials available?
- How will these total group activities be assessed, informally and formally?

Assessing During the Learning

- Are students learning the appropriate standards, skills, or content?
- Are students attentive and listening?
- Do the students exhibit a positive attitude?
- Are the students engaged in applying the information?
- Are learners retaining the information?
- Am I revamping and readjusting my plans to meet the diverse needs of my students?
- Is the time used productively?

Assessing After the Total Group Experience

- Did the students' responses show that they are learning?
- Did the props, visuals, and materials enhance learning?
- Did the teaching and learning meet the goals and expectations?
- What do the students need next?

Total Group

Disadvantages	Advantages
Difficult to manage	Directions same for all
Easy for students to get off task	Teacher directed
Difficult to differentiate	Time saved
Low level of individual participation	Students hear comments from peers

A for Alone

Assessing Before Teaching

- Who has specific gaps to be zapped according to the preassessment data?
- On which tasks do students need to work alone?
- Do I need to set up a choice board?
- Do some students need individual agendas?
- What does this student need to learn next?
- Which skills do students need to practice alone?
- How will each experience be assessed?
- What interventions are needed?

Assessing During the Learning

- Is each student challenged by the assignment(s)?
- Is each student staying on task?
- How is the learner demonstrating understanding?

Assessing After the Learning

- Did the learner complete the task(s) successfully?
- What did the student learn?
- What are the student's strengths and weaknesses?
- What do the evaluation results show?
- What does the student need next?

Alone

Disadvantages	Advantages
No opportunity to learn from others	Individual accountability
May practice incorrectly	Works at own pace
More difficult to assess each individual	Works at level of need
No interdependence	Makes individual choices
More difficult to design specific plans	Enhances independence

P for Partners

Assessing Before the Teaching

- Which assignments will be most effective in a partner working relationship?
- What is the most advantageous way to form partners?
- Is peer-to-peer tutoring needed?

- How will each partner activity be assessed?
- Is individual accountability built into the plan?

Assessing During the Learning

- Are the partners able to get along socially?
- Is each partner member contributing to the assignment(s)?
- Are partners staying on task?
- Is the assignment(s) a productive learning experience for each individual?

Assessing After the Partner Experience

- What did each partner learn?
- What does each team need to do next?
- How will partners share what they learned?
- Should these students be partners in future tasks?

Partner Sharing After the Learning Assessment: Informal

Partner activities engage all learners. When two individuals share, one student talks while the partner listens or takes notes.

Use ideas similar to the following "noteworthy note spotlights" to make partner assessments productive experiences:

- Individually write a note with two to three things you learned.
- Take your notes, and find a partner.
- Decide who will be Partner A and who will be Partner B.
- Share your notes by taking turns.

Variations

- Each partner reads all of his or her notes at one time and then chooses a favorite note to discuss.
- Partners A and B take turns, each sharing one note. Continue until all items are shared.
  - Partner A shares an item. Partner B then shares one that relates to the item that Partner A read.
  - Partner A then shares a note that relates to Partner B's note. They continue taking turns until all notes are discussed.

A/B Partners: Sharing-Linking Thinking

This activity allows students to practice linking what they learned to other facts. Teachers observe the skill with which they perform this activity. Some instruction, guidance, and practice may be needed to develop this skill.

Each student individually writes two to three things learned. Students meet with their energizing partners and decide who will be Partner A and Partner B. Partner A begins by sharing facts or information. When the teacher claps, Partner B starts with Partner A's last word and continues more thoughts. When the teacher claps again, Partner A begins with the last word from Partner B and links it to other facts related to the topic.

Partners share their written statements as follows:

- Partner A shares one item.
- Partner B shares one linking item.
- Partner A shares a second item that links to Partner B's last thought.
- Partner B shares the second linking item.

This continues until the teacher gives a signal. The partners may signal the teacher when they have shared all of the statements related to things they learned. This activity is fun and challenging.

Assessing a Working Partner Team

1. Are the students following the directions?	Yes	No
2. Do they have needed materials?	Yes	No
3. Are they working toward their goal?	Yes	No
4. Are they on task?	Yes	No
5. Are they learning the information?	Yes	No
6. Is the team productive?	Yes	No
7. Are they working cooperatively?	Yes	No
8. The partner's best work occurs when _____.		
Comments About the Experience		
Partner A Reflections		
Partner B Reflections		
Teacher Comments		

Working With a Partner

Disadvantages	Advantages
Shared ownership of a product	Provides opportunities for engagement
Difficult to assess individual work	Fosters student-focused learning
Off-task socializing	Builds trust
May not carry equal workloads	Meets interpersonal needs

S for Small Groups

Small groups work effectively when all members cooperate to complete the task. Each team member has specific tasks for individual accountability.

Assessing Before the Teaching

- What are the standards and skills to be learned?
- Which activities will be best for small-group instruction?
- Will the groups be selected by skills, randomly, alphabetically, or by interest?
- Will this be a cooperative-learning or a small-group activity?
- How will each group member be held accountable?
- How will each group session be assessed?
- What role will the individuals have?
- Is the small-group arrangement the most effective way to teach the information?
- Are the materials accessible?
- Are the directions clear and precise?

Assessing During the Learning

- Is each group member participating?
- Are team members getting along?
- Is each learner doing his or her part?
- Are group members staying on task?
- What else does the team need?
- Are group members learning the content?

Assessing After the Small Group Experience

- Was the group work worth the time?
- What did the group accomplish?
- What will you do differently next time?
- How will group members share what they learned?
- Where can the group display the product?
- How will the activity be assessed?

Small Group

Disadvantages	Advantages
Opportunities for learners to be off task	Combines views and ideas
Individual accountability is difficult	Focuses on cooperation
Unequal sharing of responsibilities	Teaches tolerance
May create power struggles	Fosters active student learning
Often dominated by one or two students	Meets interpersonal needs

EVALUATING GROUP WORK

Figure 10.4 is an example of an assessment for analyzing the success of a group member. It may be completed by the student, a peer, the group, or the teacher.

Figure 10.4 Group Member Assessment Checklist				
Name(s) _____ Date _____				
Observable Behavior	Not yet	Sometimes	Most of the time	Comments
Stayed on task				
Followed directions				
Showed respect for group members				
Completed his or her share of the work				

Use the scales in Figure 10.5 to evaluate a group. This assessment is designed to be completed by the total group, a group member, or the observing teacher.

Figure 10.5 Evaluating Group Work

Name(s) _____ Task _____

☐ Self   ☐ Peer   ☐ Group   ☐ Teacher

A. Effective use of time

I   2   3   4

B. Task performance

I   2   3   4

C. Productivity

I   2   3   4

D. Contribution Level

I   2   3   4

E. Overall summary

I   2   3   4

Comments

Independent Members Score the Group

Provide one copy of Figure 10.6 to each group member. After scoring each item, the student writes a comment to validate his or her rationale for giving a particular score.

Figure 10.6   Scoring Individuals in Group Discussion

Assignment/Task_____

Score an individual group member using the 1–4 scale.

Name of Group Members	A. Effective Use of Time	B. Task Performance	C. Productivity	D. Contribution Level	E. Overall Summary

Comments

_____

_____

_____

_____

Observer's Signature _____   Date _____

Self-Assessment for a Group Member

The checklist in Figure 10.7 is designed to help each group member to think about his or her participation, contributions, and teamwork during the assignment. Select items from the checklist that are appropriate to the situation.

Figure 10.7   Self-Assessment for a Group Participant

Name of Activity _____ Date _____

Student _____ Rater _____

1. I contributed to my group.	Yes	Sometimes	No
2. I helped others if I could, and they needed me.	Yes	Sometimes	No
3. I listened to the discussion.	Yes	Sometimes	No
4. I respected other members of my group.	Yes	Sometimes	No
5. I shared my ideas.	Yes	Sometimes	No
6. I felt that my ideas were accepted.	Yes	Sometimes	No
7. I encouraged others.	Yes	Sometimes	No
8. I was treated with respect.	Yes	Sometimes	No

A. Our group was great because

B. We needed to improve

C. Other suggestions and comments are

Signature _____ Date _____

GROUP DISCUSSION: ASSESSMENT

Observe the learner during formal and informal group discussion sessions. Identify the learner's needs and best efforts. Many times during group discussions, one student dominates the conversation. Occasionally, it is important to listen without contributing to the discussion. As the accuracy and depth of the information is observed and analyzed, identify who contributes each segment. A learner may not contribute to the discussion because he or she does not have an opportunity or has a fear of being wrong.

Observe the following aspects of a discussion scene to assess a learner's interactions:

- Contributes to the discussion
- Makes relevant and accurate contributions
- Makes a connection between information learned and personal experiences
- Refers to information learned to support a view, opinion, or comment
- Discusses the information fluently
- Draws appropriate conclusions and inferences
- Expresses opinions and ideas freely

Group Design

Use various flexible grouping designs in diverse ways to organize students for assessment tasks. Assess the situation and tasks frequently to plan the most productive learning opportunities. Change groups as needed.

Use the following statements and questions as guidelines to make flexible grouping decisions:

- The most productive grouping design for this task is _____.
- Do I need to use the same design for all learners, or should I use different designs to meet an individual student's needs?
- What are the most effective working teams for this assignment?
- Who is working with whom?
- What are the needed roles?
- Where is the best place for each group to work?
- How will the roles be assigned to the groups?
- What rules, directions, and guidelines need to be established?
- What materials will each group need to complete the tasks?
- What worked well the last time I grouped these students in working teams?

Choose the grouping design based on the standard and the purpose. Assign the students based on their individual needs. Analyze the task and the amount of time needed to complete it.

Select from a variety of grouping designs when planning assessment activities. Use knowledge-based groups, interest groups, ability groups, random groups, peer-to-peer tutoring, cooperative groups, or multiage groups to work on specific skills, review information, or learn new concepts.

Consider the following grouping scenarios to differentiate formative assessment.

Knowledge-Based Groups

Knowledge-based groups are formed according to each student's background and previous experience with the topic or skill. The learner's knowledge is determined using one or more preassessment tools. The results identify the student's readiness or entry level for a particular study. During the preassessment analysis, the student's trouble spots are pinpointed and addressed in instructional plans. This grouping design is selected to teach the standard or skill and expand each member's knowledge base. The individual student's learning potential increases when he or she is challenged on the appropriate level for success.

Interest Groups

There are several techniques to use in forming interest groups. Students can sign up for their favorite topics in a unit of study. The results of interest inventories and surveys can be used to make group assignments. When a student demonstrates an interest in a subject, he or she will usually "buy in," or have a strong desire to study and work in a group with interest-related materials and resources.

Ability Groups

Ability grouping is a traditional grouping design. Evidence of a student's ability is gathered from preassessment. The individual is grouped with learners on the same ability level.

At one time teachers formed ability groups at the beginning of the year, and those students stayed together in the group for the entire school year. Often group names such as bluebirds and redbirds were used. Once a student was assigned to a group, the learner was frequently trapped at that level with the assigned label. Educators referred to this dilemma saying, "Once a buzzard, always a buzzard."

Today, ability groups are formed as needed to teach specific skills and concepts. With flexible grouping, the student moves to a more challenging group when information and skills are mastered.

Random Groups

If a task can be easily completed by all class members, random grouping is the way to go. Choose one of the following ideas to create a novel, random grouping design:

- Count off students using numbers 1 through 7 to form seven groups. The students who are 1s work together, the 2s work together, and so on.
- Select names from a hat to form each group.
- Mix Match: Choose four or five topics. Write three or four pieces of information about each topic on separate cards. Ask students to find classmates in the room who have information about the same topic to form groups.

- Make cards using animals, objects, numerals, shapes, or colors and place the words to match them on separate cards. Ask each individual to draw a card and form a team with classmates who have a matching card.
- Draw strings. Choose five colors of yarn, and cut each into equal pieces. Place the strings in a bag. Have each individual reach into the bag and take out one piece of string. Students form groups with the matching colors.

Peer-to-Peer Tutoring

This grouping design works best when students respect each other and get along socially. Often a peer team is formed because one student has a stronger knowledge base or ability. The other student needs to learn or work more with the information. One learner teaches or tutors a classmate. Be careful not to overuse a student as a tutor. The student who knows the information needs time to learn more about the topic with extension and enrichment activities.

Tutoring sessions must be beneficial for both students. The best peer tutor is the student who has had a "light bulb" moment saying, "Now I understand it!" This individual is excited to share or teach this information. Teaching information crystallizes learning in the mind: "If I teach it, I learn it!"

Cooperative Groups

Cooperative teams are formed to complete a common task. Each team member has a role with at least one responsibility to carry out during the group work. The members have shared power and are individually accountable for the assigned responsibility. The group or team uses consensus to make decisions. Teams who work together several times create bonds, develop respect, and build team spirit. Have a discussion session with students related to the social outcomes as well as the cognitive development and learning expected from cooperative teams.

Multiage Groups

In multiage groups, an older student is paired with a younger student. This design works well if the students have an opportunity to create bonds and develop mutual respect. Often students have to be explicitly taught how to work together. Model and discuss cooperation in detail. Practice in mock simulations. Over time, the students usually develop a good working relationship in which both learners share responsibility in discussions and tasks.

Multiage groups are effective because the younger student often looks up to the older student as an academic and social role model. The older learner develops confidence and a sense of responsibility and pride.

A multiage group may be composed of students of different ages to participate in an activity, a discussion, a task, or a project. Group members may be selected by common interests, academic needs, or random selection. These groups work in multiage classrooms, with buddy classes, or across grade levels.

TROUBLESHOOTING TOOLS FOR GROUP ASSESSMENT

If negative or inappropriate behavior occurs during a group assessment, it must be corrected quickly and quietly to avoid interrupting the work of other students. The following ideas are designed as troubleshooting tools to use during group assessment activities.

What to do when a student does the following:

Acts Negatively Most of the Time

- Brainstorm positive words and phrases.
- Model appropriate comments and responses.
- Smile and show your approval when positive behavior is observed.
- Engage the student in pleasant friendly conversation about the problem, and come to solutions.
- Volunteer to be a sounding board for complaints so you solve the problems together.

Says or Does Something With Which You Do Not Agree

- Listen to the student's opinion, and remain open.
- Express your point of view in a friendly, neutral way.
- Remember that a dictator approach using "your way or the highway" will not lead to mutual understanding.

Has a Personality Clash With a Group Member

- Consider separating students, if the behavior is long term.
- Schedule a conference, and provide tips for the students to work it out together.
- Acknowledge the student's preference to work alone. Coach the student in ways to work with others when it is necessary.
- Design assignments that give each group member at least one responsibility.
- Discuss the value of positive, appropriate behaviors at the end of activities.

Has to Be "Spoon-Fed" Information

- Identify how the individual learns best. Use the student's strengths to build confidence.
- Give directions in smaller increments or "chunks."
- Use specific praise for growth and improvement.

SUMMARY

Adding an intriguing strategy is exciting and challenging for the teacher and students as they move toward differentiated learning and assessment. Before introducing a new idea, read and reread the related material. Choose the assessment tools to use. Identify challenging areas, and decide how to address each one. Then step bravely into the new learning and formative assessment format.

DIFFERENTIATED INSTRUCTIONAL PLANNING MODELS

11

Essential Question: How is formative assessment data used in planning models to facilitate and guide the process of designing differentiated instruction?

As emphasized throughout this resource, formative assessment is an evolving, ongoing process. This chapter investigates and tackles strategic planning for differentiated instruction based on assessment data. This is essential in meeting the diverse needs of learners. A model is an effective curriculum planning tool based on the gathered information. This addresses students' identified needs as they are continually targeted for mastery learning. This chapter presents the following planning models: Adjustable Assignment, Curriculum Compacting, Academic Contract, Project-Based, and Problem-Based.

ADJUSTABLE ASSIGNMENT MODEL

Adjustable assignments are strategically placed in the overall plan for the unit to challenge learners based on their needs determined by the assessment data. This model is called the tiered model in Carol Ann Tomlinson's work. We call this the Adjustable Assignment Model. The new name was chosen because in planning a teacher is constantly adjusting the assignment (Gregory & Chapman, 2007). Also, a teacher can adjust assignments for two groups, so it is not always necessary to plan a tiered assignment. A three-level adjustable assignment is developed for three identified groups who need different learning experiences. The following explanation labels and categorizes the criteria for each of the three levels of an adjustable assignment (Chapman & King, 2008). The members of the group are forever changing, fluid, and flexible. A student may have mastered one standard so for the independent assignment this learner will be placed in Level III, curriculum fast-forwarding. This same student can be assigned to a Level I assignment for a skill or standard that needs more interventions or curriculum rewinding. At other times, this same learner will be assigned to a grade level task. Each learner is assigned to the appropriate group by the data from a strategically planned assessment. This fine-tuning instruction is based on the individual needs of the learners.

Level I: Curriculum Rewinding

If assessment data reveal that students do not have the appropriate background and skills to learn the information, their intervention needs may be met by a curriculum rewinding assignment. Results of an informal or formal preassessment identify the "gaps in the learning" or the skills and information a student needs to learn next. The teacher decides the best way to provide experiences on a learner's readiness level. We refer to this as the "green for growing" group.

Using a strong preassessment activity, identify students who need more assistance in learning a particular skill or standard. These students may lack prior experience and basic knowledge to work on this skill, standard, or objective. Intervene with opportunities to work on the fundamentals required for a specific topic or skill on their grade level. They must be brought up to the readiness level for the new information so it becomes possible for effective learning to occur.

Often teachers do not feel responsible for basic information or skills students did not master in the previous grade. Teachers have so many standards to teach in the subject areas for their grade levels that there is no time to go back and reteach to meet the needs of these students. When it is obvious students cannot move to new learning without the basics or prior knowledge, a way must be found to provide the foundation they need. All students must be prepared to learn!

Level II: Grade Level

The assessment data reveal that this group of learners has the proper background and foundation to learn the grade level material being introduced. This group has the yellow label and is "a ray of sunshine" to the teacher because they are eager beavers for learning the new material. The student-focused assignment gives a learner a chance to work with the new learning. Monitoring grade level assignments serves as a valuable assessment check to identify what is understood and a need for intervention or assistance.

Level III: Curriculum Fast-Forwarding Level

This group of learners has the proper knowledge base of background experiences and already knows the grade level material being introduced. This "fired-up" group uses the red label. The teacher-focused lesson is a review for this group. It is important that they are a part of the initial class instruction and engaged during the total class lesson. Then specific designed tasks are assigned to this group to enhance, enrich, and challenge. When a learner knows one skill, it does not indicate that he or she is on this level for the next standard or skill. The placement decisions are based on assessing the mastery of each concept.

There are procedural steps to follow that simplify the planning of an adjustable assignment. Each aspect of this plan is based on ongoing formative assessments and the results gathered from the data. Here is a suggested guideline to plan these vital steps. (Chapman & King, 2008).

Step 1. Assess the Upcoming Learning

    a. Administer a formative assessment to find out what the students know about a new topic, unit, standard, concept, or skill.

    b. Interpret the data and place learners in the three adjustable assignment levels.

Step 2. Plan an Adjustable Assignment for Student-Focused Learning

    a. Fold a piece of paper into a tri-fold and label the sections Level I, II, III. See Figures 11.1 and 11.2.

Figure 11.1   Grid for Adjustable Assignment Planning

Standard _____   Formative Assessment Tool _____

Level I: Curriculum Rewinding Activity for Student Focused Assignment	Green: *Growing!*	Time _____
Level II: Grade Level Activity for Student Focused Assignment	Yellow: *Ray of Sunshine!*	Time _____
Level III: Curriculum Fast-Forwarding Activity for Student Focused Assignment	Red: *All Fired Up!*	Time _____

Figure 11.2   Example of Adjustable Assignment Planning for Mathematics

Standard: Renaming in Subtraction   Formative Assessment Tools: *Pretest and Observation*

Level I: Curriculum Rewinding   Green: *Growing!*

Student Focused Assignment Time: 15 Minutes

Draw the subtraction problems from the green mystery box, and work the problems on a blank piece of paper.

The problems have no renaming steps. They emphasize basic subtraction. The students may use manipulatives.

(Continued)

Figure 11.2 (Continued)

Level II: Grade Level   Yellow: *Ray of Sunshine!*

Student Focused Assignment Time: 15 Minutes

Draw the subtraction problems from the yellow mystery box, and work the problems on a blank piece of paper.

The problems have renaming subtraction problems.

Level III: Curriculum Fast-Forwarding   Red: *All Fired Up!*

Student Focused Assignment Time: 15 Minutes

Draw the subtraction problems from the red mystery box, and work the story problems on a blank piece of paper.

The story problems have renaming subtraction problems.

    b. Identify and write the standard, skill, or concept for the lesson and the assessment tool used at the top of the page.

    c. Write the time allotted for these assignments. All three assignments occur simultaneously; therefore, the time allotted for completion of each task is the same. In other words, they are completed in the same block time frame. Write the student-focused assignments that will challenge learners in each of the three levels.

    d. Gather materials needed for each assignment.

Step 3. Carry Out the Plan in the Classroom

    a. Teach the new standard to all learners in a novel, challenging way.

    b. Engage all students in a guided practice.

    c. Assign the student-focused assignments to the appropriate learners identified in the interpretation of the data.

    d. Move around among the groups answering questions, assessing learners, intervening, and making adjustments as needed.

    e. Celebrate the success of the learning experience.

Dual-Leveled Adjustable Assignment

If the formative assessment data reveal the need for only two assignments, use the dual-leveled adjustable assignment grid as in Figure 11.3. Plan two activities that fit two different levels to meet the differentiated needs. Design interesting engaging assignments that any student is willing to complete. Each task needs to be challenging, a quality learning experience, and a valuable use of instructional time. Plan both assignments to take the same amount of time to complete since the students work on them during the same time slot.

Figure 11.3   Dual-Leveled Adjustable Assignment

Standard: Identifying Main Idea and Supporting Detail

Assessment Tool: Rubric

Level I	Level II
1. Work with a partner. Read the first paragraph of an assigned passage. 2. Come to consensus on the main idea. Record it on the graphic organizer. 3. Go on a scavenger hunt and identify supporting details. Come to consensus and write the answers on the chart. 4. Complete as many paragraphs as time allows.	1. Work with a partner. Each partner writes a paragraph with a main idea and supporting details. 2. Partner A reads his or her own paragraph to Partner B. 3. The partners come to consensus on the main idea. They place Partner A's main idea on the chart. 4. Partners go on a scavenger hunt for Partner A's supporting details. They place findings on the chart. 5. Repeat the process for Partner B's writing.

<table>
<tr><td colspan="2">

Main Idea	Supporting Details
A.	1.
	2.
	3.
	4.
B.	1.
	2.
	3.

</td><td>

Main Idea	Supporting Details
A.	1.
	2.
	3.
	4.
B.	1.
	2.
	3.

</td></tr>
</table>

Analyze the planned adjustable assignment to assure productive use of learner time with the sample checklist provided in Figure 11.4.

Figure 11.4   Adjustable Assignment Checklist

❏ A learner is placed in a group for an assignment based on interpretation of formative assessment data.

❏ Each assignment addresses the same identified standard(s).

❏ The adjustable assignment is placed in an agenda folder.

❏ Do not adjust every assignment. Often the entire class is assigned the same task.

❏ Color-coding assignments is used to help students know which task to complete.

❏ Use flexible grouping based on learner needs.

Preassessment: The Key to Adjustable Assignments

In the study of a topic, standards are the focus of instruction. Each student has a different knowledge level related to the standard. A great challenge for the teacher is to customize instruction for the various entry levels of the students. The adjustable assignment model identifies individual levels of readiness for the standard, topic, or skill. This allows the teacher to plan instruction within the range of students' abilities, interests, and knowledge levels. The plan is designed to address a range of criteria, varying levels of difficulty, and quantities of information. The adjustable assignment model accommodates identified individual student needs.

Pinpointing needs helps the teacher identify areas where the student must "zap the gaps" in the learning, or target instruction to fill in the background information the student or group missed (see Figure 11.5). This is a critical component of instructional planning (Chapman & King, 2008).

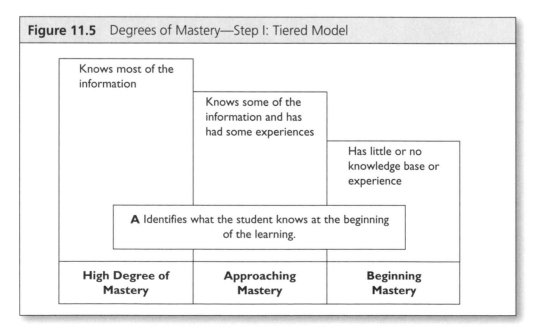

Figure 11.5   Degrees of Mastery—Step I: Tiered Model

Knows most of the information

Knows some of the information and has had some experiences

Has little or no knowledge base or experience

A Identifies what the student knows at the beginning of the learning.

| **High Degree of Mastery** | **Approaching Mastery** | **Beginning Mastery** |

In Step II, analyze what the group on each level knows. Make a specific list. Design or select the preassessment activity that will reveal the student's knowledge level, interests, background, and attitude (see Figure 11.6). Take time to discover the essential pieces. Find the best interventions for students to overcome these learning hurdles. Prepare students for the next steps in learning.

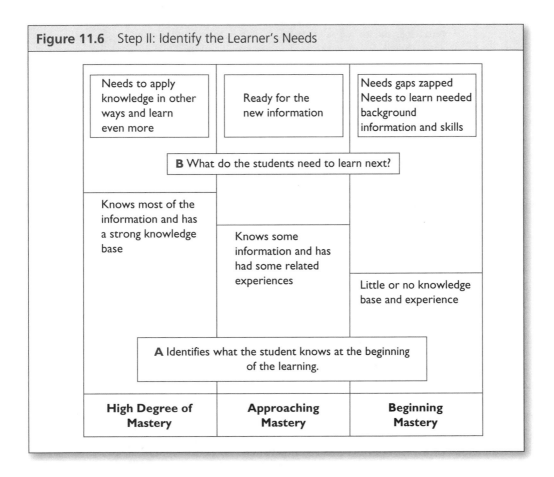

Figure 11.6 Step II: Identify the Learner's Needs

| Needs to apply knowledge in other ways and learn even more | Ready for the new information | Needs gaps zapped Needs to learn needed background information and skills |

B What do the students need to learn next?

Knows most of the information and has a strong knowledge base

Knows some information and has had some related experiences

Little or no knowledge base and experience

A Identifies what the student knows at the beginning of the learning.

| **High Degree of Mastery** | **Approaching Mastery** | **Beginning Mastery** |

In Step III, the authors, Chapman and King (2009b), have added the "how-to" section to each level (see Figure 11.7). Before completing this section, assess the learner, the plan, and the instruction. Use the results to plot the how-to section as you see the assessment questions cross all mastery levels of the differentiated learners. These assessments are necessary steps because the answers will be different in each case.

Planning With the Adjustable Assignment Model

The teacher analyzes a student's work to identify the level of intervention and instruction the individual's needs to reach personal learning goals and standards. To

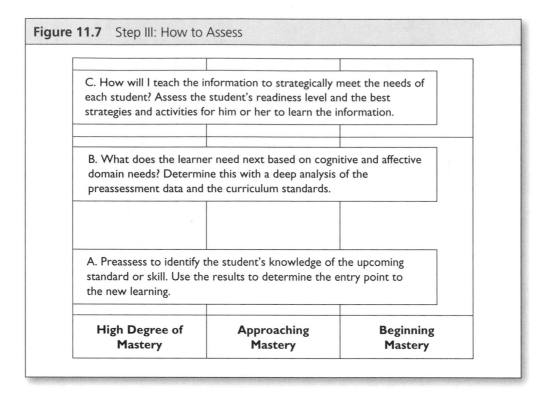

Figure 11.7   Step III: How to Assess

C. How will I teach the information to strategically meet the needs of each student? Assess the student's readiness level and the best strategies and activities for him or her to learn the information.

B. What does the learner need next based on cognitive and affective domain needs? Determine this with a deep analysis of the preassessment data and the curriculum standards.

A. Preassess to identify the student's knowledge of the upcoming standard or skill. Use the results to determine the entry point to the new learning.

| High Degree of Mastery | Approaching Mastery | Beginning Mastery |

guide instruction in a differentiated classroom, the teacher assesses the student before, during, and after the learning (see Figure 11.8).

Try the following steps:

A. View and Assess

  1. Analyze what is happening.

  2. Determine what the student knows.

The student may know the information or know how to use a particular skill but keep this knowledge well hidden. The learner may not be aware of what he or she knows about the topic. There may be a lack of focus or concentration. For example, the student may not recognize a new term as it is introduced or may not be able to link prior knowledge with the new learning situation.

When the learner cannot tell or write about a new term or topic, the student may be able to show what he or she knows by using a preferred modality, style, or intelligence. This calls for an alternative assessment such as showing it, acting it, drawing it, or using it in a real-life situation. Use a personalized assessment tool to give the student more than one opportunity to respond. This is not a waste of time because valuable information is gathered when assessment tools are customized for the learner.

B. Gather Information and Diagnose.

   1. Note the student's reaction and behaviors during learning.

   2. Examine causes for the actions or lack of response. Why is the individual showing excitement or reluctance during the learning?

C. Explore Options

   1. Pinpoint the learner's strengths and weaknesses.

   2. Identify the next steps by examining learner needs for intervention, grade-level instruction, or enrichment activities.

D. Teach and Assess

   1. Use various instructional and assessment strategies and activities to meet the student's needs.

   2. Continue the formative assessment cycle.

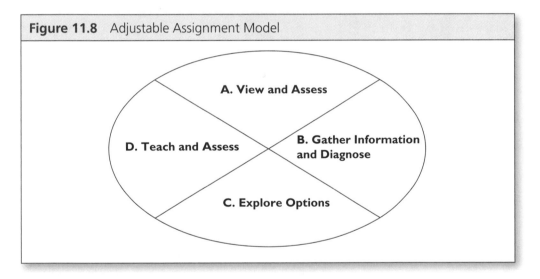

Figure 11.8 Adjustable Assignment Model

CURRICULUM COMPACTING MODEL

The Curriculum Compacting Model is used when the student knows the upcoming material. Dr. Joseph Renzulli named seven strategies that allow all learners to continue growing and learning in the areas of their greatest strengths. Dr. Renzulli first named curriculum compacting as a way to reach the academically talented. Curriculum compacting is based on his research and belief that there must be alternative programs available to learners labeled *gifted*. Figure 11.9 shows Dr. Renzulli's seven strategies.

A customized instructional plan is designed to extend or enrich learning experiences for that particular individual. This permits the student to skip portions of the curriculum that he or she knows (Reis & Purcell, 1993). This model presents seven different ways for the learner to work with the information.

Figure 11.9   Strategies for Curriculum Compacting

1. Provide an open-ended assignment.	Give learners opportunities to use higher-order thinking and creativity. Make personal links and connections.
2. Create opportunities for collaboration.	Plan in-depth assignments with partners and small groups. Combine students from other classrooms to form working cluster groups.
3. Use an adjustable assignment.	Create lessons on the learners' level of success. Give students choices.
4. Allow learners to pursue independent projects.	Give independent studies. Pose questions to explore, research, and solve. Give the problem-solving model as a project.
5. Provide the appropriate books and resources.	Select fiction and nonfiction books below, on, and above grade level with student input, if possible. Provide opportunities for students to choose challenging and inviting resources.
6. Implement an accelerated program as needed.	Accelerate content to keep students engaged and challenged. Permit students to skip standards, skills, grades or subjects as indicated by the data.
7. Aim for deep enrichment schoolwide.	All learners need a challenge. Provide exciting, challenging activities for everyone.

Source: Adapted from Renzulli (2008).

Use a variety of work samples and preassessments to identify the student who does not need to sit through the next instructional teaching segment, subject, or class. If the individual has demonstrated that he or she already knows the information and can apply the learning elsewhere, the student is ready for an independent activity or class assignment. If the activities are boring, the student may be nonproductive, and the time will be wasted! The Curriculum Compacting Model gives the learner opportunities to increase his or her knowledge base and excel.

The Curriculum Compacting Model was originally designed for students who needed a form of accelerated learning. In the following adaptations of the model, it is used with students who need foundation knowledge and experiences before they are introduced to the current lesson. When assessment reveals that a student knows the material and can apply, interpret, and adapt the information to real-life situations, the Curriculum Compacting Model can be used to plan activities that interest the student and motivate him or her to learn more about the topic or concept. This student has an extensive knowledge base and is ready to learn more and to dig deeper into the topic. The learner is ready to move on to a new concept, skill, or subtopic. Offer the individual choices related to the study, send him or her to another teacher's class to be challenged, or design a contract with the student that requires the use of higher-order thinking skills or more challenging materials. This method avoids placing a cap on an individual's potential.

Ways to Use Curriculum Compacting

Curriculum compacting can be set up in various ways. This is based on need, conversation with the adult team, and coming to the conclusion that this is the best educational plan for the learner at the time of the decision.

Compacting Scenarios for Individual Students

- Tasks are selected, adjusted, and paced to meet the individual's needs.
- The learner goes to another room to be challenged.
- A student selects or is assigned a project to complete.
- The student and teacher design a contract for a challenging task.
- The learner works with higher-order thinking skills that are challenging and interesting.

The following scenario illustrates the importance of using curriculum compacting in differentiated instruction. Preassessment data and teacher observation revealed that one individual in math class knew so much about the lessons that the student could teach the Pre-Algebra class. Out of boredom, this student exhibited inappropriate behaviors and an "I don't care" attitude. This behavior affected personal performance and the performance of classmates. The learner was moved from a middle school Pre-Algebra class to a high school Algebra I class. After one week of leaving the middle school and joining the Algebra I class, the student's attitude and performance in all academic subjects improved because this student was academically challenged and successful. As seen in this example, a curriculum compacting assignment is carried out at a specific time to meet the personal needs of an identified student.

Grade-Level Curriculum Compacting

The following Curriculum Compacting Model is designed for a class with a diverse knowledge base related to a unit. The focus is on the group that needs enrichment, enhancement, and challenging activities to further develop higher-level skills and knowledge base on a topic. Each learner proves that the targeted standard is mastered. The members of this group of learners are determined by the preassessment test results and teacher observation.

This teaching scenario also benefits the students on and below grade level. Their specific needs are similar and can be targeted and addressed accordingly. Group membership changes based on the results of the ongoing assessment data. This is an example of knowledge-based flexible grouping. Follow these steps to carry out the plan:

1. Designate one teacher as the focus teacher.

2. Target a topic of weakness.

3. Give a pretest of the skills to all students.

4. Record scores from high to low of all the learners from all the grade level classes on one compiled list.

5. Select the students with the top twenty scores in the classroom to work with the focus teacher during the period dedicated to the topic.

6. The remaining students disperse heterogeneously among the other grade-level teachers for the standard, unit, or topic of study.

7. Have the students go to the designated classes each day during the focus period.

8. Give a posttest to assess individual progress and needs.

ACADEMIC CONTRACT MODEL

An academic contract is a written work agreement between a teacher and a student that facilitates differentiated instruction. The learner has the opportunity to select a task of interest related to the current standards, concepts, or skills targeted during the topic of study. Often, the contract is created by the student. In the agreement, the student presents his or her ideas for working with the information in his or her own way. The teacher reviews the contract, makes suggestions, and meets with the student for final approval. This may take place in a student–teacher conference. An academic contract is effective when the assignment challenges the student's mind and expands the knowledge base related to the standard using productive thinking.

An Academic Contract That Works

Differentiating assessments with contracts assure student accountability in the following ways:

- The teacher and student develop a list of tasks and activities to be completed with specific requirements.
- The student completes the contract within a specific time frame.
- Tasks and activities are modified to the learner's readiness level and interests.
- The student selects tasks that engage his or her areas of strengths.
- The academic contract appropriately enhances knowledge in the current study.
- The assignment is designed for the learner to complete successfully with little adult supervision.
- The task teaches or reinforces grade level standards, concepts, or skills.

Student Contract Request Form

Develop the academic contract request form with a timeline and the student's plan mapped out for discussion and approval before the work begins. Figure 11.10 shows a sample form. It is important that the teacher and learner understand each part of the contract. The academic contract is submitted for the teacher's approval and signature.

Figure 11.10 Academic Contract Request Form

A. Student's Request

Name _____   Date of Submission _____

My Proposal

   I. I would like to _____

   2. The time needed for completion is _____   Due Date _____

   3. Materials and resources I will need include _____

B. Teacher's Feedback

   I. _____   Teacher Approval   _____   Teacher Denial

   2. Teacher Suggestions

   3. Conference Dates

      a. Viewing the Proposal _____

      b. Progress Check _____

      c. Final Conference _____

   4. Signatures for Commitment and Acceptance

Student _____   Date _____

Teacher _____   Date _____

Comments

Assess the Value and Usefulness of the Contract

The checklist in Figure 11.11 is designed for a teacher to analyze a contract and determine its usefulness. Remember, only accept contracts when they provide appropriate, worthwhile experiences for the individual. Avoid "contractitis."

Figure 11.11   Effective Academic Contract

An Academic Contract

- ☐ Addresses the current standard
- ☐ Meets the needed objectives
- ☐ Adds worthwhile information or skills
- ☐ Meets the established timeline
- ☐ Uses the student's time wisely
- ☐ Helps the student learn how to apply time management techniques
- ☐ Allows for individual choices and interests
- ☐ Challenges the student's mind
- ☐ Can be completed without adult supervision
- ☐ Engages the student's unique strengths, talents, and interests
- ☐ Provides a sense of personal ownership
- ☐ Encourages creativity
- ☐ Develops problem-solving and thinking skills
- ☐ Provides productive learning experiences

Additional comments

_____

_____

PROJECT-BASED MODEL

A Project-Based Model provides a framework for the goals and objectives, the topic choices, the outline for the task, progress checks and assessment tools, the timeline, and the presentation format. Projects engage students in an expanded independent, partner, or small-group study on a specific topic. This model can be designed as a class project, a content-centered project, or a student-choice contract.

Before assigning a project, check to see that it is age-appropriate and that the student will be able to process the information. Design the assignment so the student is challenged but can complete each component independently. In other words, the project must be a student-centered activity, not something that an adult needs to assist or supervise directly. The teacher may monitor progress with the student's process journal or other tool to provide feedback and suggestions along the way. Create a checklist such as the following to analyze the value of the assignment. Relate the assignment to information or skills the student must learn at that grade level or in the content area.

Ask the following questions:

- Will the project meet the student's needs?
- Is the project a wise use of the learner's time?

- Do the activities enhance the student's understanding of one or more curriculum standards?
- Can the students meet the requirements as designated on the timeline?

Assess the Project-Based Model Assignment

Select the appropriate standard, objective, or benchmark for the content information and grade level. Use the questions in Figure 11.12 to assess the appropriateness of the project-based assignment before it is presented to the student. If "no" is a response to one or two questions, examine the value of the assignment. If three or more responses are "no," abandon the assignment and replace it with another project that meets the criteria. If all responses are "yes," the assignment is a valuable learning experience.

Figure 11.12 Preassessing a Project: A Teacher's Checklist		
The project-based assignment is …	Yes	No
1. Developed with ongoing monitoring throughout the work.		
2. Designed within the student's level of success.		
3. Content related and relevant to the learner's needs.		
4. Designed to be completed independently.		
5. Devised to engage the student in researching and processing information.		
6. Designed to fit the time frame.		
7. Providing the student experience with new learning.		
8. Filled with high-interest activities.		
9. Created with accessible resources and materials.		
10. Designed with progress checkpoints.		
11. Easily assessed with an assessment tool.		

The questions for the teacher and the student are designed to assess the feasibility of the project during the selection process. Too often the selection is made too quickly without a thorough investigation in the steps of the process. When this happens, an adult must intervene and assist the learner. The student becomes frustrated when the topic is boring, tasks are too difficult, or appropriate materials are not available. Teach the student how to use the following questionnaire. The goal of this activity is to show the learner how to carefully analyze a project before it is selected.

Preassessing a Project: A Student's Questionnaire

The student completes a preassessment questionnaire with approximately ten items. Use questions similar to the following for the learner to analyze interests, abilities, and needs related to the selected project:

- What are the most interesting subtopics of this study for me?
- Which part would make a good project?
- What do I want to learn?
- What is the timeline?
- How will I meet the requirements of the progress checkpoints?
- Where can I find the material and resources?
- What are my greatest concerns or needs related to the assignment?
- What do I need before I begin the project?
- Who do I want to be my peer evaluator or adviser?
- How will the product look when it is finished?
- How will I present the project?
- Which self-assessment tools do I need to use?
- How will my work be assessed?

Assessing a Post-Project Display

For the Teacher

When the project is completed, the teacher assesses the value of the displayed learning by using questions similar to the following:

- Did the project tasks address the content objectives and standards?
- Did the student grow in his or her knowledge base through these experiences?
- Are all parts of the project accurate?
- Does the project reflect learning over a period of time?
- Is the student able to explain the information learned?
- Will there be allotted time for the student to present the project?
- Would this project be beneficial for another learner?

For the Student

When the student completes a project, he or she assesses the value of the work using reflective prompts similar to the following:

- Was this learning experience worth the time I spent on it? Why or why not?
- I learned . . .
- Where did I need more direction?
- I am proud of the following tasks . . .
- Which tasks needed more time to complete?
- My deepest thinking was used when . . .
- I want to know more about . . .
- If I could select another project, it would be . . .

Using a Project Timeline

Each student has his or her own project assignment. Assign each participant a project partner to assess and brainstorm ideas for support and improvement. Partner teams meet on the due dates listed on the timeline. Each learner shares information related to the progress of his or her individual project. See Figure 11.13. This keeps learners from completing the project at the last minute and helps them pace their time wisely. This learning procedure emphasizes the thinking and problem-solving techniques involved in the project process. Too often the emphasis is mainly placed on the product.

Figure 11.13   Project Progress Timeline

Student's Name _____

Items	Due date	Completed
1. Submit the selected topic.	_____	_____
2. Share your plan for the project.	_____	_____
3. List identified materials and needed resources.	_____	_____
4. Bring in research reference notes.	_____	_____
5. Share an outline of the research paper.	_____	_____
6. Read a rough draft of the paper.	_____	_____
7. Brainstorm ideas for the presentation.	_____	_____
8. Select a way to present the material.	_____	_____
9. Read the final paper.	_____	_____
10. Rehearse the presentation.	_____	_____

Student's Signature _____

Partner Signature _____

PROBLEM-BASED MODEL

The problem-based model makes learning more meaningful and applicable to the real world. Select problems that intrigue and engage learners. Topics may be related to environmental issues, health problems, abuse, taxation, global warming, or other local and national concerns. Usually only one question or problem is developed and posed to the class. Whenever appropriate, differentiate by providing opportunities for students to select the problem. Ask for their suggestions and input about the processes and procedures they will use to solve the problem or answer the essential question. Learners become proactive detectives, investigators, scientists, or inventors when they play a role in the decision-making process.

Examples

- How can traffic flow be improved at the intersection near the recreation center?
- What can be done to prevent littering on the grounds of our school?

Assessing the Problem Choice: A Teacher's Questionnaire

- Is the problem worth the time?
- Do the assignment and activities enhance the content and standards required at this grade level?
- Is it age appropriate?
- Will the results be observable for the learner(s)?
- Are materials and resources accessible?
- How will individual roles and tasks be assigned?
- What checkpoints and self-assessment tools will be used?
- How will I assess the individuals or groups?
- Do the learners understand the assessment process?

Guidelines for Choosing the Problem: A Student's Questionnaire

The following questionnaire is designed to guide the thinking processes of individuals, small groups, or total class in selecting a problem:

- What problem will be investigated?
- Will the results make a difference?
- What information and research are needed?
- How will the needed information be gathered?
- What materials and resources are needed?
- How will the results be compiled?
- What procedures are needed to solve the problem?
- What checkpoint or self-assessment tool will be used?
- How will the teacher assess my work?
- How will the information and solutions be presented?

SUMMARY

Models provide a framework for detailed planning to accommodate the diverse needs of students. They are planning tools that are driven by and based on careful analysis of assessment data. Selecting the right model to use at the appropriate time is the key!

PLANNING FOR DIFFERENTIATED ASSESSMENT 12

The object of education is to prepare the young to educate themselves throughout their lives.

—Robert Maynard Hutchins

Essential Question: What are the most effective ways to use formative assessment to organize and plan differentiated assessment?

Formative assessment data drive the instructional planning. Selecting the most productive tool provides the essential information for strategic planning to meet the individual needs of each learner. A treasure trove of formative assessment tools are used before, during, and after the learning.

STEP UP TO FORMATIVE ASSESSMENT PLANNING

Be consciously aware of the assessment strategies and tools embedded in instruction. The following step-by-step procedure is provided for using ongoing assessment data in planning. The accompanying discussion ideas, following each step, are intended to serve as a guide to implemente formative assessment in daily plans. Figure 12.1 contains a condensed version of this procedure to further explain the plan.

Remember, if you fail to plan, you plan to fail!

Adapt the following implementation plan for formative assessment to meet the needs of your students:

1. **Identify what to teach.**
   - Choose the unit of focus.
   - Select what you are going to teach.
   - Identify the standard, concept, topic, benchmark, or skill to assess.

2. **Select the assessment tool and preassess the students.**

   - Determine how to preassess the learner's knowledge base.
   - Identify the tool(s) to use.
   - Is the tool an informal or formal assessment?
   - Does the assessment need to address the affective domain, the cognitive domain, or both?
   - Identify the student's knowledge base, interests, and attitudes.
   - What does the student know about the topic at the beginning of the study?
   - What are the student's attitudes and feelings related to the topic?

3. **Compile and analyze the preassessment data.**

   - Compile the data from the preassessment to gather information about the learner's past experiences and background. If the learner's prior knowledge and experiences are positive, the student usually has a yearning to learn more. In a positive state, the student's mind resembles a sponge, ready to absorb the information. New learning builds on the emotions and feelings developed from past experiences with related opportunities. If the student sees a need for it and perceives the information or skill as meaningful, relevant, and interesting, learning occurs. If the student has had bad experiences or difficulties with previous information in the area of study, mental barriers need to be removed. It is important to be aware of past experiences to build on the learner's foundation of knowledge, attitudes, and desires.
   - Determine and examine the skills or information the student needs to learn next.
   - Fill in the learning gaps that may be barriers to understanding. Too often this important step in planning is omitted. Start the student at his or her current knowledge base and move along the learning continuum, according to the student's individual needs. Fill in the gaps.
   - If the student has the needed background and knowledge, assign grade-level activities.
   - Educators have been heard to remark, "You are in the _____ grade," "You should know this," or "You were suppose to learn this in _____ grade." When it is obvious that a student missed important information, move the learner from where he or she is and build the foundation for learning with specific interventions. It is up to the teacher to make this happen. The best time for any student to gain knowledge or skills missed is now. Remember, it is never too late to learn.

4. **Brainstorm a quantity list of activities.**

   - Prepare a list of all the instructional strategies and activities that can be used to teach the information. This generates a quantity list of strategies with a large number of options from which to choose. This process is very effective when teams of teachers brainstorm the list. Each teacher uses the list to select the most engaging and appropriate activities. These strategically chosen activities and strategies create effective, approaches with quality to teach the information.

5. **Lay out the plan.**
   - Determine the most effective and efficient order for teaching the activities, concepts, and strategies.
   - Examine the lesson plan sequence for flow, relevance, and need.

6. **Assess the plan.**
   - Check the plan for providing differentiated strategies by labeling targeted intelligences and learning styles of the activities and strategies in your lesson plan. This gives opportunities for learners to work with the information in their own ways.
     o Examples:
        V/L—verbal/linguistic
        M/R—musical/rhythmic (see multiple intelligences in Chapter 4)
        A—auditory, V—visual, K—kinesthetic
   - Fix the "Big *O*s," the overkills and omissions. When the labeling is complete, decide if there are too many activities under one intelligence target. For example, if a math unit, standard, concept, or benchmark is planned, check to see if most of the activities target the logical/mathematical intelligence. If so, refer to the original brainstormed list to find activities or strategies that target other intelligences. If a way of learning is omitted, think of an effective approach to teach the information or refer to the original list of activities and strategies.
   - Select the appropriate flexible grouping designs.
        T = Total Group   A = Alone   P = Partner   S = Small Group
   - Label each activity in the plan by using T, A, P, or S. Ask yourself if students are working alone and with others through the study to create an appropriate blend of group scenarios. For example, if the students work on the activity in a small group, and then work with the information alone, label this activity "SA" for small group and alone.
   - Decide how and when to use student self-reflection and assessment activities.
   - Incorporate celebration events in the learning plan.

7. **Teach.**
   - Be aware of individual and group needs. Whenever possible, provide immediate feedback and guidance to avoid gaps in learning.
   - Decide if you need to revamp, review, reteach, move on, enrich, or enhance the learning.
   - Identify and omit boring parts and frustrating points with challenging opportunities.
   - Use the self-reflection and assessment opportunities while constantly interpreting formative assessment and evaluative data.

8. **Strategically readjust the plan.**

9. **Assess after the learning.**
   - Administer evaluations to determine growth and needs.
   - Celebrate learning.

- Ask yourself questions similar to the following to guide new instructional plans.
  - Which students mastered the skills, standards, or objectives?
  - How will I reach the needs of learners who need interventions and other accommodations?
  - What do students need to learn next?
  - What can be carried over to the upcoming unit?
  - What will I teach next?

Figure 12.1   Using Ongoing Assessment in Planning

9. Assess After the Learning
Identify the information and skills the student learned. Ask, "What does the student need next?" Use this information to set new instructional goals.

8. Strategically Readjust the Plan
During instruction revisit, revamp, and adjust the plan to meet individual's needs.

7. Teach the Students
Continue to monitor and assess student learning with strategically planned formative assessment tools. Assess before and during the learning.

6. Assess the Plan
Label selected activities with targeted intelligences or learning styles. Analyze the flexible grouping designs to be sure they create an accurate flow of movement. Provide opportunities for students to work alone and with others.

5. Lay Out the Plan
Choose the best strategies and activities from the brainstormed list for the particular student or group. Design a quality plan for instruction that meets the learner's identified needs and interests.

4. Brainstorm a Quantity of Activities
List all possible activities and strategies to teach this information to the individual or group of students to meet the specific needs identified in the data analysis.

3. Compile and Analyze the Preassessment Data
Examine and interpret the data. Use the gathered information to identify the learner's needs and entry points for instruction.

2. Select the Assessment Tool and Preassess the Students
Find out what the individual learners know. Identify their prior knowledge, interests, and experiences related to the upcoming information.

1. Identify What to Teach
Identify the specific standard, skill, indicator, or benchmark to teach. Set goals.

CONTENT, PROCESS, PRODUCT, AND LEARNING DISPOSITION ASSESSMENT

According to Carol Ann Tomlinson (1999), there are at least three components working hand in hand in a differentiated classroom: (1) content, (2) process, and (3) product. She identifies these as commonalities to differentiate for learning and therefore assess. We added the student's learning dispositions, a category that includes attitude, habits of mind and work, and abilities—all of the elements that make up the holistic learner. We have added disposition as a major area for assessment because of its profound influence on the results. We place assessment as the centerpiece. Teachers assess the content, how the student processes the information, and how the product shows evidence of what the student has learned. The teacher can use the chart in Figure 12.2 to plan assessments for these elements.

Figure 12.2 Content, Process, Product, and Learning Disposition Assessment

Tool	Content	Date	Process	Date	Product	Date	Learning Dispositions	Date
Anecdotal Records								
Center Activities								
Computerized Programs								
Conferences								
Conversations								
Demonstrations								
Inventories								
Journal Entries								
Likert Scales								
Literary Circles								
Logs								
Metacognitive Questions								
Observations								
Portfolios								
Presentations								
Projects								
Reports								
Rubrics								
Standardized Tests								
Surveys								
Teacher-Made Tests								
Text Talks								
Topic-Related Activities								

Content Assessment Tools

Content assessment tools gather evidence of the knowledge, progress, understanding, and growth that occur during the teaching of a unit, topic, or standard. For example, a unit portfolio is a content assessment tool because it consists of work samples gathered throughout a topic of study. It provides evidence of the student's growth and needs related to his or her understanding of the standard, content, skill, or information.

Examples

- What have you learned about the country you studied?
- Read a book, article, or brochure related to the historical time period. Which facts do you need to remember?

Process Assessment Tools

Process assessment tools reveal how evidence or data are gathered over time. The assessment tool may analyze the learner's level of engagement in specific learning. The student tells or demonstrates his or her step-by-step thinking processes. This shows how the student is mentally manipulating information. When the learner processes orally, it is easier to identify mistakes for correction and success for celebration. This procedure reveals the learner's unique and personal way of approaching problems and situations.

Process assessment tools answer the following question during the planning phase of instruction: How will the students learn this information?

Examples

- Tell how you got the answer.
- Show each step. Explain what you did on each step. Why?

Product Assessment Tools

Product assessment tools are administered at one time and create a result that can be examined. For example, when a rubric is presented as a guideline at the beginning of a project assignment, the student and teacher know and understand the expectations and requirements of the assignment. The score is based on the product or evidence gathered.

Examples

- Create a rap, rhyme, or jingle to describe the new geometric shapes.
- Design a travel brochure for the country of _____.

Learning Disposition Assessment Tools

Learning disposition assessment tools gather evidence about the student's attitudes, feelings, behavior, and interests. For example, an individual checklist in a cooperative learning activity records a team member's social interactions and level of participation.

Examples

- I was a contributing team member when I _____.
- The most difficult aspects of working with the group.

The Full Planning Toolbox

Use Figure 12.4 on pages 188 to 192 to select the appropriate tools for planning differentiated assessment.

You may choose to use the same tool at different times for different purposes. Place a check mark by each assessment activity in your current toolbox indicating when the tool was used. Add planning notes as needed.

THE ROLE OF FORMATIVE ASSESSMENT IN CURRICULUM PLANNING

Formative assessment plays a major role in curriculum planning. The gathered information informs and guides long- and short-term lesson development. Various assessment sources provide evidence for curriculum decisions. For example, use a product, observations, a test, a conference session, and a portfolio to develop effective plans.

Analysis of assessment results highlights individual student strengths and needs. This in-depth view reveals how much learners can do successfully, how much they know, and their levels of understanding. Use this valuable information to identify the next steps for designing personalized strategies and activities.

Looking at the Student

A. View and Assess

Describe the student. Include the student's attitudes, interests, preferred ways to learn, strengths, and weaknesses.

B. Gather Information and Diagnose

Explore the information collected.

What does this work tell about how the student learns best?

What are the learner's characteristics or behaviors influencing performance?

What factors outside the classroom might impact the student's performance?

C. Explore and Select Options for Strategies and Activities

Based on the learner's past performance, which strategies and activities do I plan to better meet the needs of this student?

Which students will benefit from this activity?

D. Teach and Assess

Implement high-energy presentations of the selected tailored activities and strategies.

Constantly monitor and use appropriate interventions to make adaptations to the learner's personal needs.

Looking at Learning Goals, Objectives, and Expectations

A. View and Assess

Identify the objectives, goals, and standards.

Did the results meet expectations?

Did it meet the standard requirements?

B. Gather Information and Diagnose

Identify the skills, standards, and knowledge learned?

What revamping, interventions, and enhancements worked?

What did not work?

C. Explore and Select Options for Strategies and Activities

Does this piece of work show evidence that objectives were met?

D. Teach and Assess

Identify the information or skills that need reteaching, more practice, and further explanation.

Detect mastered standards and skills.

Examine the successful segments that worked.

Looking at a Work Sample

A. Observe and Gather Data

What does the work tell me?

What does the student understand or not understand?

B. Analyze the Information and Diagnose

What are the learner's accomplishments toward meeting the standard goals?

What can I learn from the data to accelerate the student's growth?

Which information does the student understand? What can the student do?

What do I need to plan next?

C. Explore and Select Options for Strategies and Activities

Identify the standard or skill that needs more work.

What needs more explanation?

Determine the gaps remaining in the understanding.

When and how do I need to revisit, review, or spiral this skill or information?

D. Teach and Assess

What did the student learn?

What does the student need to learn next?

Looking at the Learner's Prior Experiences and Background Knowledge

A. Observe and Gather Data

What background knowledge or prior experience is evident from examining the student's work?

B. Analyze Information and Diagnose

Examine experiences that interfere with this student's learning?

What prior knowledge does this student need to enhance learning progress?

Did the learner make personal links and connection to the new information?

C. Explore and Select Options for Strategies and Activities

How did the student's prior experiences or background knowledge promote better understanding?

How can I fill in the gaps?

D. Teach and Assess

What experiences can I add to this part of the teaching?

How is the student's knowledge base expanded?

What does the student need to learn next?

Looking at the Teacher

A. View and Assess

What does this piece of work reveal about the teaching approach?

Were the student's intelligences and learning styles considered?

Were clear directions provided?

Were appropriate materials available?

How were the students motivated to tackle the assignments?

B. Gather Information and Diagnose

Why was this assignment chosen for this particular student?

What other questions do I have as I look at this work?

Is the mastery of objectives evident?

C. Explore and Select Options for Strategies and Activities

Which strategies, assignments, and activities worked? How?

How can assignments be improved?

Which portions of the lecturette were effective?

D. Teach and Assess

How effective was the plan?

What do I need to do next?

What additional information do I need to accommodate this learner?

How will I acquire the information, resources, and materials?

Source: Adapted from Goff, Colton, and Mohlman Langer (2000).

ESSENTIAL QUESTIONS FOR PLANNING

The central function of assessment, therefore, is not to prove whether or not teaching or learning have taken place, but to improve the quality of teaching and learning, and to increase the likelihood that all members of society will acquire a full and critical literacy.

—NCTE/IRA Standards for the Assessment of Reading and Writing

Effective teachers cannot be satisfied with a minimum competency or level of mastery learning. The "sit, get, spit, and forget" approach to learning, in which students sit at their desks, get the information, spit it back on the test, and then forget it, does not benefit students. Teachers may say, "I taught this information!" but the essential question is, "Did the students learn the information and transfer it to long-term memory for immediate application?" This and related questions help educators stay on track.

For Teachers and Students

What is the standard, concept, essential question, or benchmark?

What is the purpose or objective?

For Teachers

What do I expect my students to know?

How will I know the learner knows the information?

How am I going to preassess the knowledge?

How am I going to document or record my findings?

What directions do I need to give?

For Students

What do I know?

What am I supposed to know?

How can I show what I know?

What are the directions?

Do I understand each step of the task?

What do I want to learn about this?

What are my goals?

Which parts are going to be the most interesting?

Which segments of the study do I dread?

What questions do I have?

Assess the Assessment Tool

Did this assessment instrument provide a positive experience for students?

Were the students actively engaged in the tasks?

Did the questions uncover the students' knowledge base, prior experiences, and abilities?

Did students understand the directions?

Do specific items need clarification?

Were the assessment tasks within each student's range of success?

TEACHING ASSESSMENT STRATEGIES

Introduce each new assessment strategy so everyone understands the term(s) and the process before using it. This alleviates fear of the unknown and presents assessment as an integral part of learning. See the examples in the suggested guideline that follows. Each step is designed to generate thinking about the many ways to present assessment.

1. Identify the assessment strategy or tool.

2. Write the name of the assessment strategy in large colorful letters on a chart or poster. Use an appealing writing style or unusual fonts to make the visual unique.

3. Pronounce the strategy's name.

4. Ask the student to echo or repeat the pronunciation.

5. Explain the purpose of the strategy and its usefulness as a lifelong tool for learning.

6. Give examples of how this strategy will benefit the student.

7. Lead a discussion about how people apply this assessment strategy in their careers and daily living.

8. Model the steps in the strategy.

9. Teach the learner to ask the question, "How am I going to remember this assessment strategy?"

For example, follow the previous steps, and demonstrate how the think-aloud strategy is used to talk through a thinking or problem-solving process. Verbalize your inside thinking processes with each step so students can hear your thoughts as you work through the procedures. According to Davey (1983), the think-aloud technique enhances thinking as the learner visualizes, connects ideas, monitors understanding, and finds solutions.

EFFECTIVE DIFFERENTIATED ASSESSMENT PRACTICES

As you move forward in differentiating or coaching others, keep in mind the following summary to guide the use of differentiated assessment tools to identify the learner's needs and strengths for strategic planning.

The Chapman and King Dozen: Differentiated Formative Assessment

1. Use a variety of preassessment tools to identify the learner's knowledge base and prior experiences.

2. Design specific plans based on formative assessment results.

3. Strategically assess students before, during, and after learning.

4. Involve the learner in intriguing and engaging assessment activities and strategies.

5. Continually monitor and use effective interventions.

6. Use flexible grouping strategies to optimize learning.

7. Use a variety of assessment tools.

8. Plan assessment activities to produce successful experiences for the learner.

9. Teach learners to create and apply self-assessment strategies.

10. Provide immediate feedback and assistance.

11. Emphasize individual growth.

12. Celebrate success.

The Institute of Education Sciences provides scientific-based research for the U.S. Department of Education (Hamilton et al., 2009). The guide on using achievement data presents five practical recommendations for educators (see Figure 12.3). Use the questions in professional development sessions and adapt the suggestions for implementation.

Figure 12.3   Applying Formative Data

Recommendations	Questions to Assess Use of Assessment Data	Suggestions for Implementation
1. Make data part of an ongoing cycle of instructional improvement.	• Are formative data used to guide and customize instructional plans? • What strategies and activities are used to collect formative data before, during, and after instruction? • How are data shared with students? Parents? • What communication strategies are used periodically to stress the value of using ongoing assessment? • How are data used to drive decision making in the classroom, school, and district?	• Use formative data collection and analysis to guide planning for differentiated instruction. • Make data collection an integral part of instruction. • Use assessment data to design strategic customized plans for the unique needs of learners. • Share the benefits of using ongoing assessment data to students and parents. • Emphasize the value of using data to save time while meeting unique needs of all learners. • Use collected data to make constructive decisions.
2. Teach students to examine their own data and set learning goals.	• How is a positive assessment climate established to engage learners? • What terms do my students need to discuss and interpret data? • Which self-assessment tools can students use before, during, and after learning? • How can I engage learners in interpreting and discussing assessment results? • What activities can students use to make corrections and improvement to feedback?	• Establish a positive assessment climate that engages learners in the data-gathering process. • Introduce students to the assessment lingo they will hear and use. • Teach learners how to use a variety of self-assessment tools. • Guide learners to use ipsative assessment, which involves using the data to set their personal learning goals. • Use a variety of self-assessment tools that provide immediate feedback.

(Continued)

Figure 12.3 (Continued)

Recommendations	Questions to Assess Use of Assessment Data	Suggestions for Implementation
3. Establish a clear vision for schoolwide data use.	• Do I build in enough assessment tools for my formative and summative gathering? • In our school, is it expected that assessment guides planning? • What do we need as a culture to better assess learning? • How do we apply data to benefit and develop productive learners?	• Inform each stakeholder of the value of using formative and summative assessments to identify the student's needs. • Use standards-based curriculum planning. • Incorporate the learner's learning styles, intelligences, preferences, talents, and interests as a vital component of the learner's profile. • Guide all stakeholders to view assessment and instruction as an inseparable expectation for teaching and learning. • Use assessment to guide planning in daily work as well as in long-term goals. • Use data-driven decision making as an integral part the school culture.
4. Provide supports that foster a data-driven culture within the school.	• Is time scheduled for reading, discussing, and sharing data? • What type of professional development is provided? Needed? • Do educators take responsibility for the problems revealed from assessment data?	• Establish time for collaborative teams to examine and interpret data. • Provide time for planning that is based on data interpretation. • Collect and share data with stakeholders. • Brainstorm ways to improve instruction for learners with specific problems.
5. Develop and maintain a district-wide data system.	• Does the district gather and share data with each school? • Does the community have educators who have access to the information? • Do educators know how to use the data? • Are schools' comparative data shared with educators? • Are teachers from different schools and/or grade levels given time to brainstorm and share ideas of ways to improve and teach the needed information?	• Establish a procedure to present the analyzed data to each faculty or subject area team. • Continually keep educators updated and trained on the latest technology to access and analyze assessment data.

Source: Adapted from Hamilton et al. (2009).

GENERATE CHANGE FOR DIFFERENTIATED FORMATIVE ASSESSMENT

- Provide on-going professional development to create a treasure trove of effective assessment tools.
- Routinely survey the staff's needs and interests to identify next steps in professional learning.
- Establish mutual goals.
- Collaborate, share, plan and work together.
- Develop a common language to understand the terms, acronyms, and jargon related to formative differentiated assessment.
- Develop focus teams to analyze and share best practices for on-going assessment.
- Generate trust and acceptance for each team member.
- Share resources and ideas.
- Provide time to interpret and analyze assessment data to plan differentiated instruction.
- Brainstorm and showcase individual, classroom assessment accomplishments.
- Celebrate! Celebrate! Celebrate!

SUMMARY

We offer the following acronym as a reminder to strategically apply formative differentiated assessment strategies and tools:

Analyze individual strengths and needs.

Strategically plan for each learner to improve and excel.

Set a positive tone for assessment.

Explore abilities and utilize strengths.

Supply assistance and appropriate materials.

Stress resilience and self-efficacy.

Monitor for immediate intervention.

Empower learners with self-directed assessment strategies.

Nurture and support individual efforts and growth.

Translate needs and strengths into active learning.

Refer to the components of this acronym while assessing and planning to develop lifelong metacognitive learners.

Figure 12.4   Planning Toolbox for Formative Assessment: Strategies and Activities

Formative Assessment Tools and Strategies	Page Number	Use Now	In Progress	Not Yet	Planning Comments
Chapter 1 **One Tool Doesn't Fit All: Introduction**					
Defining Assessment Terms	3				
Differentiated Assessment Analysis	5				
Assessment in the Age of Accountability	6				
Benefits of Differentiated Assessment Strategies	10				
Teacher's Role in Differentiated Assessment	11				
Chapter 2 **Research and Best Practices**					
Processing Information and Memory	15				
Memory Obstacles and Prescriptions	16				
Develop Intelligent Behaviors for Assessment	20				
Authentic Assessment	23				
Performance Feedback	24				
Chapter 3 **Creating a Climate for Formative Assessment**					
Affective Domain	26				
Emotions	26				
Self-Efficacy	28				
Motivation for Assessment	29				
Physical Climate	32				
Yuk Spots/Bright Spots—Scavenger Hunt	33				
Setting Climate Goals	35				
Assessment of the Classroom Environment	36				
Chapter 4 **Knowing the Learner**					
Information Gathering	39				
Gardner's Multiple Intelligences	42				
Exploring Goleman and Sternberg	47				
True Colors	50				

Formative Assessment Tools and Strategies	Page Number	Use Now	In Progress	Not Yet	Planning Comments
Through Animals' Eyes	49				
Student Perception	50				
Ways of Knowing and Showing	53				
Surveys	54				
Observation Tips	56				
Chapter 5 Self-Assessment					
Self- Talk	59				
Teaching Self-Assessment	63				
Self-Checking Techniques	64				
Assessing on-Task behaviors	67				
Chapter 6 Formative Assessing Before the Learning					
Engaging Students Before Learning	72				
Ponder and Pass	73				
Signal and Action Response	73				
Take a Stand	73				
Knowledge Base Corners	74				
Content Knowledge Boxes	76				
Personal Surveys and Inventories	78				
Brainstorming	78				
Color Clusters	78				
Gallimaufry Gathering	79				
ELOs	80				
Pre-Test	81				
Standardized Test Data	82				
Chapter 7 Formative Assessment During the Learning					
Observation	84				
Anecdotal Assessment	84				
Know it! Show It!	86				
Response Cards	87				
High Five	90				
A Bump in the Road	91				

(Continued)

Figure 12.4 (Continued)					
Formative Assessment Tools and Strategies	*Page Number*	*Use Now*	*In Progress*	*Not Yet*	*Planning Comments*
Color Coding	91				
Sketches From the Mind	91				
Analyzing Student Notes	91				
Checkpoint Tests	92				
Daily Grades	92				
Chapter 8 **Formative Assessment After the Learning**					
Effective Questioning Techniques	94				
Bloom's Taxonomy: Defining the Lingo	95				
Post Sharing Celebrations	96				
Likert Scales	97				
Rubrics	97				
Checklists	104				
Assessing Reading and Writing Skills	107				
Using Assessment Combinations	109				
Design Delights	111				
Assessing With Journals	111				
Graphic Organizers	113				
Prompts for Assessments	114				
Assessing With a Blank Page	114				
Performance Assessment	114				
Teacher-Made tests	115				
Portfolios	118				
Chapter 9 **Differentiating Summative Assessment**					
Standardized Assessment	123				
Creating a Positive Testing Environment	125				
Give Effective Directions	125				
Teach Test-Taking Skills	126				
Grading	127				
Parent Conferences	128				
Chapter 10 **Assessment for Differentiated Instruction and Flexible Grouping**					
Technology Software	131				

Formative Assessment Tools and Strategies	Page Number	Use Now	In Progress	Not Yet	Planning Comments
Performance Assessment Technology	132				
Technology-Based Assessment Tools	133				
Assessment Cubing	133				
Choice Boards	134				
Assessment Agendas	136				
Stations, Centers, Learning Zones for Assessment	138				
Assessment for Flexible Grouping	140				
Total Group	141				
Alone	142				
Partner	142				
Small Groups	145				
Assessing Group Discussions	149				
Troubleshooting Tools Group Assessment	152				
Chapter 11 **Differentiating Instruction Planning Models**					
Adjustable Assignment Model	155				
Curriculum Compacting Model	163				
Academic Contract Model	166				
Project-Based Model	168				
Problem-Based Model	171				
Chapter 12 **Planning for Differentiated Assessment**					
Implementation Plan	173				
Content Assessment Tools	178				
Process Assessment Tools	178				
Learning Disposition Tools	178				
Role of Assessment in Curriculum Planning	179				
Essential Questions for Planning	182				
Teaching Assessment Strategies	183				
Effective Differentiated Assessment Practices	184				
Making Change for Differentiated School Success	187				
Assessment Tools and Strategies at Work	188				

We hope the formative assessment models, strategies, and tools in this book will assist and support you and all dedicated educators. Empower each student to be a metacognitive, self-directed learner every day. Add the treasure trove of ideas to your formative assessment toolbox collection. Differentiate assessment techniques remembering that *one tool doesn't fit all!*

—Carolyn and Rita

BIBLIOGRAPHY

Airasian, P. W. (2011). *Classroom assessment* (7th ed.). New York: McGraw-Hill.

Assessment. (2010). *New Oxford American Dictionary, 3rd edition.* Oxford Press: New York.

Bloom, B. S., & Krathwohl, D. R. (1956). *Taxonomy of educational objectives: The classification of educational goals. Handbook I: Cognitive domain.* New York: Longman, Green.

Caine, R., & Caine, G. (2005). *Brain/mind learning principles in action: The fieldbook for making connections, teaching and the human brain.* Thousand Oaks, CA: Corwin.

Campbell, D. (2000). Authentic assessment and authentic standards. *Phi Delta Kappan, 81*(5), 404–407.

Chapman, C., & King, R. (2008). *Differentiated instructional management: Work smarter, not harder.* Thousand Oaks, CA: Corwin.

Chapman, C., & King, R. (2009a). *Differentiated instructional strategies for reading in the content area* (2nd ed.). Thousand Oaks, CA: Corwin.

Chapman, C., & King, R. (2009b). *Differentiated instructional strategies for writing in the content area* (2nd ed.). Thousand Oaks, CA: Corwin.

Chapman, C., & King, R. (2009c). *Test success in the brain-compatible classroom* (2nd ed.). Thousand Oaks, CA: Corwin.

Costa, A. L. (2008). *The school as a home for the mind: Creating mindful curriculum, instruction, and dialogue.* Thousand Oaks, CA: Corwin.

Davey, B. (1983). Think aloud: Modeling the cognitive processes of reading comprehension. *Journal of Reading, 27,* 44–47.

DeBono, E. (1999). *Six thinking hats* (2nd ed.). Boston: Back Bay Books.

Gardner, H. (2011). *Multiple intelligences: The unschooled mind: How children think and how schools should teach* (3rd ed.). New York: Basic Books.

Goff, L., Colton, A., & Mohlman Langer, G. (2000). Power of the portfolio. *Journal of Staff Development, 21*(4), 48.

Goleman, D. (1995) *Emotional intelligence.* New York: Bantam Books.

Goleman, D. (2006). *Emotional intelligence: 10th anniversary edition: Why it can matter more than IQ.* New York: Bantam Books.

Gregory, G., & Chapman, C. (2007). *Differentiated instructional strategies: One size doesn't fit all* (2nd ed.). Thousand Oaks, CA: Corwin.

Hamilton, L., Halverson, R., Jackson, S., Mandinach, E., Supovitz, J., & Wayman, J. (2009). *Using student achievement data to support instructional decision making* (NCEE 2009–4067). Washington, DC: National Center for Education Evaluation and Regional Assistance, Institute of Education Sciences, U.S. Department of Education. Retrieved from http://ies .ed.gov/ncee/wwc/publications/practiceguides/

Hattie, J. (1996). *Self-concept*. Hillsdale, NJ: Erlbaum.

Kounin, J. S. (1970). *Discipline and management in classrooms*. New York: Holt, Rinehart, and Winston.

Levine, M. (2002). *One mind at a time*. New York: Simon & Schuster.

Marzano, R. J. (2000). *Transforming classroom grading*. Alexandria, VA: Association for Supervision and Curriculum Development.

Marzano, J. (2010). *Formative assessment & standards-based grading: Classroom strategies that work*. Bloomington, IN: Marzano Research Laboratory Powered by Solution Tree.

Marzano, R. J., Pickering, D. J., & Pollock, J. E. (2001). *Classroom instruction that works: Research-based strategies for increasing student achievement*. Alexandria, VA: Association for Supervision and Curriculum Development.

Popham, W. J. (2010b). *Everything school leaders need to know about assessment*. Thousand Oaks, CA: Corwin.

Reis, S. M., & Purcell, J. H. (1993). An analysis of context elimination and strategies used by elementary classroom teachers in the curriculum compacting process. *Journal for the Education of the Gifted, 16,* 147–170.

Renzulli, Joseph. Teach to the Top. *Instructor*. March/April, 2008. Vol 117 Issue 5.

Routman, R. (2000). *Conversations: Strategies for teaching, learning, and evaluating*. Portsmouth, NH: Heinemann.

Silver, H. F., Strong, R. W., & Perini, M. J. (2000). *So each may learn: Integrating learning styles and multiple intelligences*. Alexandria, VA: ASCD.

Sousa, D. (2006). *How the brain learns* (3rd ed.) Thousand Oaks, CA: Corwin.

Stepanek, M. (2002). *Heartsongs*. New York: Hyperion Press.

Sternberg, R. J. (1997). *Thinking styles*. New York: Cambridge University Press.

Stiggins, R. (2011). *An introduction to student-involved assessment FOR learning* (6th ed.). Boston: Addison Wesley

Sylwester, R. (2000). Unconscious emotions, conscious feelings. *Educational Leadership, 58*(3), 20–24.

Tileston, D. W. (2004). *What every teacher should know about student assessment*. Thousand Oaks, CA: Corwin.

Tomlinson, C.A. (1999). *The differentiated classroom: Responding to the needs of all learners*. Alexandria, VA: Association for Supervision and Curriculum Development.

Tomlinson, C., & McTighe, J. (2006). *Integrating differentiated instruction and understanding by design: Connecting content and kids*. Alexandria, VA: Association for Supervision and Curriculum Development.

Vygotsky, L. S. (1978). *Mind in society*. M. Cole, V. John-Steiner, S. Scribner, & E. Souberman (Eds.). Cambridge, MA: Harvard University Press.

Wiggins, G. (1999). *Assessing student performance*. San Francisco: Jossey-Bass.

INDEX

Note: Page numbers in italics refer to charts and figures.

CORWIN

A SAGE Company

The Corwin logo—a raven striding across an open book—represents the union of courage and learning. Corwin is committed to improving education for all learners by publishing books and other professional development resources for those serving the field of PreK–12 education. By providing practical, hands-on materials, Corwin continues to carry out the promise of its motto: **"Helping Educators Do Their Work Better."**